The Ordeal of Change

Books by Eric Hoffer

The True Believer

The Passionate State of Mind

The Ordeal of Change

The Temper of Our Time

Working and Thinking on the Waterfront

First Things, Last Things

Reflections on the Human Condition

In Our Time

Before the Sabbath

Between the Devil and the Dragon

Truth Imagined

The Ordeal
of Change

Eric Hoffer

Hopewell Publications

Published by Hopewell
Publications, LLC
PO Box 11, Titusville, NJ
08560-0011 (609) 818-1049

info@HopePubs.com
www.HopePubs.com

Library of Congress Cataloging-in-Publication Data
Hoffer, Eric.
    The ordeal of change / Eric Hoffer.
        p. cm.
    Originally published: New York : Harper & Row, 1963.
    Includes index.
    ISBN 1-933435-10-0 (alk. paper)
    1. Social change. 2. Communism. 3. Intellectuals.
4. History--Philosophy. I. Title.
    HX36.H6 2006
    303.4--dc22

                                    2006011379

First Edition

Printed in the United States of America

Photographs taken from the Hoffer estate private archives

To Lili and all the Osbornes

The greatest thing in the world is
to know how to belong to oneself.

\- Michel de Montaigne

Contents

The remarkable thing is that it is the crowded life that is most easily remembered. A life full of turns, achievements, disappointments, surprises, and crises is a life full of landmarks. The empty life has even its few details blurred and cannot be remembered with certainty.

— Eric Hoffer

1 · Drastic Change

It is my impression that no one really likes the new. We are afraid of it. It is not only as Dostoyevsky put it that "taking a new step, uttering a new word is what people fear most." Even in slight things the experience of the new is rarely without some stirring of foreboding.

Back in 1936 I spent a good part of the year picking peas. I started out early in January in the Imperial Valley and drifted northward, picking peas as they ripened, until I picked the last peas of the season, in June, around Tracy. Then I shifted all the way to Lake County, where for the first time I was going to pick string beans. And I still remember how hesitant I was that first morning as I was about to address myself to the string bean vines. Would I be able to pick string beans? Even the change from peas to string beans had in it elements of fear.

In the case of drastic change the uneasiness is of course deeper and more lasting. We can never be really prepared for that which is wholly new. We have to adjust ourselves, and every radical adjustment is a crisis in self-esteem: We undergo a test; we have to prove ourselves. It needs inordinate self-confidence to face drastic change without inner trembling.

The simple fact that we can never be fit and ready for that which is wholly new has some peculiar results. It means that a population undergoing drastic change is a population of misfits, and misfits live and breathe in an atmosphere of passion. There is a close connection between lack of confidence and the passionate state of mind and, as we shall see, passionate intensity may serve as a substitute for confidence. The connection can be observed in all walks of life. A workingman sure of his skill goes leisurely about his job and accomplishes much though he works as if at play. On the other hand, the workingman new to his trade attacks his work as if he were saving the world, and he must do so if he is to get anything done at all. The same is true of the soldier. A well-trained soldier will fight well even when not stirred by strong feeling. His morale is good because his thorough training gives him a sense of confidence. But the untrained soldier will give a good account of himself only when animated by faith and enthusiasm. Cromwell used to say that common folk needed "the fear of God before them" to match the soldierly cavaliers. Faith, enthusiasm, and passionate intensity in general are substitutes for the self-confidence born of experience and the possession of skill. Where there is the necessary skill to move mountains there is no need for the faith that moves mountains.

As I said, a population subjected to drastic change is a population of misfits—unbalanced, explosive, and hungry for action. Action is the most obvious way by which to gain confidence and prove our worth, and it is also a reaction against loss of balance—a swinging and flailing of the arms to regain one's balance and keep afloat. Thus drastic change is one of the agencies which release man's energies, but certain conditions have to be present if the shock of change is to turn people into effective men of action: there must be an abundance of opportunities, and there must be a tradition of self-reliance. Given these conditions, a population subjected to drastic change will plunge into an orgy of action.

The millions of immigrants dumped on our shores after the Civil War underwent a tremendous change, and it was a highly irritating and painful experience. Not only were they transferred, almost overnight, to a wholly foreign world, but they were, for the most part, torn from the warm communal existence of a small town or village somewhere in Europe and exposed to the cold and dismal isolation of an individual existence. They were misfits in every sense of the word, and ideal material for a revolutionary explosion. But they had a vast continent at their disposal, and fabulous opportunities for self-advancement, and an environment which held self-reliance and individual enterprise in high esteem. And so these immigrants from stagnant small towns and villages in Europe plunged into a mad pursuit of action. They tamed and mastered a continent in an incredibly short time, and we are still in the backwash of that mad pursuit.

Things are different when people subjected to drastic change find only meager opportunities for action or when they cannot, or are not allowed to, attain self-confidence and self-esteem by individual pursuits. In this case, the hunger for confidence, for worth, and for balance directs itself toward the attainment of substitutes. The substitute for self-confidence is faith; the substitute for self-esteem is pride; and the substitute for individual balance is fusion with others into a compact group.

It needs no underlining that this reaching out for substitutes means trouble. In the chemistry of the soul, a substitute is almost always explosive if for no other reason than that we can never have enough of it. We can never have enough of that which we really do not want. What we want is justified self-confidence and self-esteem. If we cannot have the originals, we can never have enough of the substitutes. We can be satisfied with moderate confidence in ourselves and with a moderately good opinion of ourselves, but the faith we have in a holy cause has to be extravagant and uncompromising, and the pride we derive from an identification with a nation, race, leader, or party is extreme and overbearing. The fact that a substitute can never become an organic part of ourselves makes our holding on to it passionate and intolerant.

To sum up: When a population undergoing drastic change is without abundant opportunities for individual action and self-advancement, it develops a hunger for faith, pride, and unity. It becomes receptive to all manner of proselytizing, and is eager to throw itself into collective undertakings which aim at "showing the world." In other words, drastic change, under certain conditions, creates a proclivity for fanatical attitudes, united action, and spectacular manifestations of flouting and defiance; it creates an atmosphere of revolution. We are usually told that revolutions are set in motion to realize radical changes. Actually, it is drastic change which sets the stage for revolution. The revolutionary mood and temper are generated by the irritations, difficulties, hungers, and frustrations inherent in the realization of drastic change.

Where things have not changed at all, there is the least likelihood of revolution.

2 · The Awakening of Asia

The tendency is to ascribe the present revolutionary turmoil in Asia to Communist agitation, or see it as an upheaval against foreign domination or misrule by corrupt native governments. Though there is a large element of truth in these views, they somehow fail to go to the heart of the matter. The nations of Asia have for uncounted centuries submitted to one conqueror after another and been misruled, looted, and bled by both foreign and native oppressors without letting out a peep. If then the masses are now rising in protest, it is not because domination and corruption have become unduly oppressive, but because the masses are not today what they were in the past. Something has happened to change their temper. We are told, it is true, that an awakening has taken place in Asia. But if this "awakening" is to be more than a metaphor, it must refer to specific changes in individual attitudes, inclinations, and aspirations. We ought to know what these changes are and how they were brought about.

The same is true of Communist agitation: its effectiveness in Asia is due less to the potency of its propaganda than to the temper of the people it tries to propagandize. When not backed by force, Communist propaganda can persuade people only of what they want to believe, and it can make headway only when it gives people something they desperately desire. It seems obvious that we cannot begin to speculate on the state of affairs in Asia unless we have a fairly clear idea of the individual attitudes, inclinations, and, above all, desires prevailing there at present. What is it that the ill-fed, ill-clad, and ill-housed masses in China, India, Indonesia, etc., so desperately desire?

Economic theory can give only a dull and unconvincing answer. One thinks of the shouting and marching, and the sea of upturned faces one has seen in newsreels and photographs—grimacing, passionate faces, each framing a gaping mouth. One wonders what is going on behind these faces and what it is that the gaping mouths shout. Do they shout for bread, clothing, and houses? Do they clamor for the good things of life? Do they call for freedom and justice? No. The clamor that is rising all over the Orient is a clamor for pride. The masses in Asia will sacrifice every economic benefit they have, and their lives too, to satisfy their craving for pride. The sea of open mouths roars defiance and not economic grievances and demands. As we shall see, this clamorous craving for pride is a characteristic manifestation of the process of awakening, and it is by probing the nature of this process that we are most likely to reach the core of our problem.

To say that the impact of the West was a chief factor in the awakening of Asia is not to say that it was oppression and exploittation by the Western colonial powers that did it. For not only are oppression and exploitation an old story in Asia, but the colonial regimes of the British in India and of the Dutch in Indonesia were fairly beneficent—more so perhaps than any regime those countries ever had or are likely to have for some time. I am convinced that were the Western colonial powers a hundred times more beneficent, and had they been animated from the very beginning by the purest philanthropic motives, their impact on the Orient would still have had the fateful consequences we are witnessing at present. For Western influence, irrespective of its intentions, almost always brought about a fateful change wherever it penetrated, and it is this change that is at the root of the present revolutionary unrest.

The change I have in mind is of a specific nature—the weakening and cracking of the communal framework. Everywhere in

Asia, before the advent of Western influence the individual was integrated into a more or less compact group—a patriarchal family, a clan or a tribe, a cohesive rural or urban unit, a compact religious or political body. From birth to death the individual felt himself part of a continuous eternal whole. He never felt alone, never felt lost, and never saw himself as a speck of life floating in an eternity of nothingness. Western influence invariably tended to weaken or even destroy this corporate pattern. By trade, legislation, education, industrialization, and by example, it cracked and corroded the traditional way of life, and drained existing communal structures of their prestige and effectiveness. The Western colonial powers offered individual freedom. They tried to shake the Oriental out of his lethargy, rid him of his ossified traditionalism, and infect him with a craving for self-advancement. The result was not emancipation but isolation and exposure. An immature individual was torn from the warmth and security of a corporate existence and left orphaned and empty in a cold world. It was this shock of abandonment and exposure which brought about the awakening in Asia. The crumbling of a corporate body, with the abandonment of the individual to his own devices, is always a critical phase in social development. The newly emerging individual can attain some degree of stability and eventually become inured to the burdens and strains of an autonomous existence only when he is offered abundant opportunities for self-assertion or self-realization. He needs an environment in which achievement, acquisition, sheer action, or the development of his capacities and talents seems within easy reach. It is only thus that he can acquire the self-confidence and self-esteem that make an individual existence bearable or even exhilarating.

Where self-confidence and self-esteem seem unattainable, the emerging individual becomes a highly explosive entity. He tries to derive a sense of confidence and of worth by embracing some absolute truth and by identifying himself with the spectacular doings of a leader or some collective body—be it a nation, a congregation, a party, or a mass movement. He and his like become a breeding ground of convulsions and upheavals that shake a society to its foundations. It needs a rare constellation of circumstances if the transition from a communal to an individual existence is to run its course without being diverted or reversed by catastrophic complications.

Europe at the turn of the fifteenth century witnessed a similar release of the individual from the corporate pattern of an all-embracing Church. At the beginning, the release was accidental. A weakened and discredited Church lost its hold on the minds and souls of the people of Europe. There, too, the emergence of the individual was less a deliberate emancipation than an abandonment. But how different were the attending circumstances then from what they are now in Asia! The emerging European individual at the end of the Middle Ages faced breathtaking vistas of new continents just discovered, new trade routes just opened, the prospect of fabulous empires yet to be stumbled upon, and new knowledge unlocked by the introduction of paper and printing. The air was charged with great expectations and there was a feeling abroad that by the exercise of his capacities and talents and with the aid of good fortune the individual on his own was equal to any undertaking at home and across the sea.

Thus by a fortuitous combination of circumstances, the fateful change from a communal to an individual existence produced an outburst of vitality that has since been characteristic of the Occident and marks it off from any other civilization. Yet even so, the transition was not altogether smooth. The convulsions of the Reformation and Counter-Reformation stemmed from the fears and passionate intensities of people unequal to the burdens and strains of an individual existence.

No such exceptional combination of circumstances attended the crumbling of communal life in Asia. There the awakening of the individual occurred in a landscape strewn with the litter and rubble of centuries. Instead of being stirred and lured by breathtaking prospects and undreamt-of opportunities, he finds himself mired in a life that is stagnant, debilitated, and inordinately meager. It is a world where human life is the most plentiful and cheapest thing, and where millions of hungry hands grab at the meanest prize and meagerest morsel. It is, moreover, an illiterate world, where even rudimentary education confers distinction and lifts a man above the common run of toiling humanity. The articulate minority is thus prevented from acquiring a sense of usefulness and of worth by taking part in the world's work, and is condemned to the life of chattering, posturing pseudo-intellectuals.

The rabid extremist in present-day Asia is usually a man of some education who has a horror of manual labor and who develops a mortal hatred for a social order that denies him a position of command. Every student, every minor clerk and office-holder, every petty member of the professions feels himself one of the chosen. It is these wordy, futile people who set the tone in Asia. Living barren, useless lives, they are without self-confidence and self-respect, and their craving is for the illusion of weight and importance, and for the explosive substitutes of pride and faith.

It is chiefly to these pseudo-intellectuals that Communist Russia directs its appeal. It brings them the promise of membership in a ruling elite, the prospect of having a hand in the historical process, and, by its doctrinaire double-talk, provides them with a sense of weight and depth.

As to the illiterate masses, the appeal of Communist preaching does not lie in its "truths," but in the vague impression it conveys to them that they and Russia are partners in some tremendous, unprecedented undertaking—the building of a proud future that will surpass and put to naught all the "things that are."

The crucial fact about the awakening in Asia is that it did not come from an accession of strength. It was not brought about by a gradual or sudden increase of material, intellectual, or moral powers, but by the shock of abandonment and exposure. It was an awakening brought about by a poignant sense of weakness. And we must know something about the mentality and potentialities of the weak if we are to understand the present temper of the people in awakening Asia.

It has been often said that power corrupts. But it is perhaps equally important to realize that weakness, too, corrupts. Power corrupts the few, while weakness corrupts the many. Hatred, malice, rudeness, intolerance, and suspicion are the fruits of weakness. The resentment of the weak does not spring from any injustice done to them but from the sense of their inadequacy and impotence. We cannot win the weak by sharing our wealth with them. They feel our generosity as oppression. St. Vincent de Paul cautioned his disciples to deport themselves so that the poor "will forgive you the bread you give them." But this requires, in both giver and receiver, a vivid awareness of a God who is the father of all, and a living mastery of the religious idiom which we of this day do not, and perhaps cannot, have in full measure. Nor can we win the weak by sharing our hope, pride, or even hatred with them. We are too far ahead materially and too different in our historical experience to serve as an object of identification. Our healing gift to the weak is the capacity for self-help. We must learn how to impart to them the technical, social, and political skills which would enable them to get bread, human dignity, freedom, and strength by their own efforts.

My hunch is that in mastering the art or the technique of helping the weak to help themselves we shall solve some of the critical problems which confront us, not only in our foreign relations, but also in our domestic affairs.

3 · Deeds and Words

There is little doubt that the Cold War has quickened the awakening and modernization that are now going on at full blast in Asia and Africa. Communist pressure is accelerating the end of colonial tutelage, and both sides in the Cold War are wooing the emerging new nations with economic and military aid and with ready recognition of their status as sovereign states.

Now, no one can gainsay the fact that in this kind of wooing the United States has not been doing too well. Our generosity, diplomacy, and propaganda have not won for us a marked measure of wholehearted adherence. Our effort, thus far, seems to lack some essential ingredient. Particularly baffling has been the petulant and often sneering response to our unprecedented outpouring of money, food, raw materials, machines, and military aid. Awkwardness or even tactlessness in our manner of giving cannot possibly explain this unexpected reaction.

Much has been written on our failure to gauge the temper and real needs of the people we try to help. It is implied that were our offering of aid comprehensive enough and our manner of giving adequate we would have the world wholly on our side. Yet the more one thinks on the subject the more one realizes that the attitude toward us is not mainly determined by the nature of our policies and our manner of giving.

The baffling response we hear does not originate in the people we try to help but in a group of self-appointed spokesmen and mediators who stand between us and the mass of people. This group is made up of university teachers and students, writers, artists, and intellectuals in general. It is these articulate people who are the source of the rabid anti-Americanism which has been manifesting itself in many countries since the end of the Second World War. One cannot escape the impression that there is a natural antagonism between these "men of words" and twentieth-century America. It is not the quality of our policies which offends them but our very existence. The intellectuals everywhere see America as a threat. Their petulant faultfinding is the expression of an almost instinctive fear, and it is of vital importance that we should understand the nature of this fear.

In almost every civilization we know of, and in Europe, too, up to the end of the Middle Ages, the equivalent of the intellectual was either a member of a ruling elite or closely allied with it. In ancient Egypt and Imperial China, the literati were a privileged part of the population. They were magistrates, administrators, and officials of every kind. In India, the uppermost caste of the Brahmins was also the caste of the educated. In classical Greece, the philosophers, dramatists, poets, historians, and artists were also soldiers, sailors, lawmakers, politicians, and men of affairs. In the Roman Empire, there was an intimate alliance between the Greek intellectuals and the Roman men of action. The Romans needed the Greek intellectual—needed him to satisfy their craving for beauty which they could not satisfy by their own creativeness, and needed him also for the management of affairs at home and in the provinces. It was this dependence on the Greek intellectual which eased the spread of Roman rule in the Hellenized part of the Mediterranean world. In Europe, too, during the Middle Ages, most of the educated people were of the clergy and hence members of an elite. But the fifteenth century, which saw the emergence of the modern Occident, also saw a fateful change in the status of the European intellectual.

The catastrophic events of the fourteenth century—the Black Death, which killed off a large part of the population and nearly half of the clergy, and the divisions and disorders of the Papacy—weakened the hold of the Catholic Church on the European masses. This in conjunction with the introduction of paper and printing made it possible for education to escape the control of an all-embracing Church. There emerged a large group of non-clerical teachers, students, scholars, and writers who were not members of a clearly marked privileged class, and whose social usefulness was not self-evident.

In the modern Occident power was, and still is, the prerogative of men of action—landowners, soldiers, businessmen, industrialists, and their hangers-on. The intellectual is treated as a poor relation and has to pick up the crumbs. He usually ekes out a living by teaching, journalism, or some white-collar job. Even when his excellence as a writer, artist, scientist, or educator is generally recognized and rewarded, he does not feel himself one of the elite.

The intellectual's passionate search for an acknowledged status and a role of social usefulness has been a ferment in the Occident since the days of the Renaissance. He has pioneered every upheaval from the Reformation to the latest nationalist or socialist movement. Yet the intellectual has not known how to retain a position of leadership in the movements and new regimes he has done so much to initiate and promote. He has usually been elbowed-out by fanatics and practical men of action. This has been particularly so in the case of the nationalist movements which have pullulated all over the Occident during the past hundred years.

These movements were usually pioneered by poets, writers, historians, scholars, and philosophers who hoped to find in the corporate warmth of the national state their rightful place as bearers of culture, legislators, statesmen, dignitaries, and men of affairs. The practical solid citizens who are now considered the pillars and guardians of patriotism, as a rule, kept shy of nationalist movements in their early stages, but moved in and took over once the movements became going concerns, and the national states began to consolidate. The intellectual was left out in the cold. He was no better off in the national state than in the dynastic state. One has the feeling that the intellectual has since tried to counter this usurpation by shifting his espousal from the national to the Socialist state

In Asia and Africa, too, the wider diffusion of literacy, due largely to Western influence, gave rise to numbers of unattached men of words. Their search for a weighty and useful life led them, as it did their counterparts in Europe, to the promotion of nationalist and Socialist movements.

Now, although the homelessness of the intellectual is more or less evident in all Western and Westernized societies, it is nowhere so pronounced as in our own common-man civilization. America has been running its complex economy and governmental machinery, and has been satisfying most of its cultural needs without the aid of the typical intellectual. Nowhere has the intellectual so little say in the management of affairs. It is natural, therefore, that the intellectuals outside the United States should see in the spread of Americanization a threat not only to their influence but to their very existence.

It is strange that when we consider the differences between our social order and that of a Communist country, we rarely refer to the striking difference in its attitude toward the intellectual. There is no doubt that the intellectual has come into his own in the Communist world. In a Communist country, writers, artists, scientists, professors, and intellectuals in general are near the top of the social ladder and feel no doubt about their social usefulness. They are the ideal of the rising generation. Czelaw Milosz says of the intellectual in the Communist countries that "never since the

Middle Ages has he felt himself so necessary and recognized." *
The people who come over to us from the Communist regimes are
mostly men of action—soldiers, diplomats, sportsmen, technicians,
and skilled workers. The intellectual, even when he can travel
outside the Communist world, rarely takes advantage of the
opportunity to escape.

The Communists have always had an acute awareness of the
fateful relations between the intellectual and the established order.
They are convinced, in the words, of Stalin, that "no ruling class
has managed without its own intelligentsia." In the Anglo-Saxon
world, social stability has been maintained without the wholehearted allegiance of the intellectuals. But, with the advent of the
Cold War, the attitude of the intellectual toward the prevailing
dispensation has everywhere become a factor in national survival.
For in a Cold War words count at least as much as deeds. Our chief
handicap in the bidding for souls that is going on in every part of
the world has been our lack of words. Our deeds could not prevent
a gang of double-talking murderers and slanderers from posturing
as saviors of humanity. Only by a masterly use of words could we
have evoked a vivid awareness of the loathsomeness of Stalin and
his work, and communicated it not only to friends and neutrals, but
to the Communists themselves.

Our men of action, however able and well-intentioned, cannot
be our spokesmen in the battle for souls. Whatever the hands that
guide our policies, the voice that makes itself heard must be the
voice of our foremost poets, philosophers, writers, artists, scientists, and professors. Only they can get around the roadblock which
bars our way to the dispirited millions everywhere. Just as in time

---

* This is not contradicted by the fact that intellectuals have been impris-
oned and liquidated in Communist countries. What the intellectual craves
above all is to be taken seriously, to be treated as a decisive force in
shaping history. He is far more at home in a society that weighs his every
word and keeps close watch on his attitudes than in a society that cares
not what he says or does. He would rather be persecuted than ignored.

of a hot war, there is an automatic rise in our appreciation of men in uniform, so in time of a cold war, there must be a general awareness of the vital role the intellectuals have to play in our struggle for survival. And they must be given a share in the shaping and execution of policies which they will be called upon to expound and defend.

4 · Imitation and Fanaticism

A t present, the modernization of a backward country is still largely a process of Westernization—the transplantation of practices, methods, and attitudes indigenous to Western Europe and America. This means that rapid modernization is above all a process of imitation, and it is legitimate to wonder whether there may not be something in the nature of imitation which renders rapid modernization so explosive and convulsive.

Contrary to what one would expect, it is easier for the advanced to imitate the backward than the other way around. The backward and the weak see in imitation an act of submission and a proof of their inadequacy. They must rid themselves of their sense of inferiority, must demonstrate their prowess, before they will open their minds and hearts to all that the world can teach them. Most often in history it was the conquerors who learned willingly from the conquered. The backward, says de Tocqueville, "will go forth in arms to gain knowledge but will not receive it when it comes to them." Thus the grotesque truculence, posturing, conceit, brazenness, and defiance which usually assail our senses whenever a backward country sets out to modernize itself in a hurry stem partly from the desperate need of the weak for an illusion of strength and superiority if they are to imitate rapidly and easily.

Communism's unquestionable appeal to backward countries avid for modernization is due only in part to the example of Soviet Russia lifting itself out of backwardness by its own efforts and in a relatively short time. More immediate and decisive is the Communists' proven ability to ready a backward society for victory on the battlefield. Though it remains doubtful whether a Communist regime can instill in the masses an enduring readiness to work, there is no doubt that it knows how to mold a backward population into an effective army, and instill it with a fanatical will to fight. The Western democracies, try as they may, cannot generate pride, enthusiasm, and a spirit of self-sacrifice in a population poignantly conscious of its backwardness and inferiority. Christianity and democracy did not take root in Asia and Africa because they did not come as instruments for the conversion of the weak into conquerors.[*] Nationalism and industrialization, two other gifts of the West, can serve such a purpose and have found a ready acceptance. It is significant that when the Jesuits first came to China to save souls, they were asked by the Emperor to cast cannon and were made masters of ordnance.

Seen as a process of imitation, it becomes understandable why the Westernization of a backward country so often breeds a violent antagonism toward the West. People who become like us do not necessarily love us. The sense of inferiority inherent in the act of imitation breeds resentment. The impulse of the imitators is to overcome the model they imitate—to surpass it, leave it behind, or, better still, eliminate it completely. Now and then in history the last was done first: the imitators began by destroying the model and then proceeded to imitate it. We are apparently most at ease when we imitate a defeated or dead model.

It is of course to be expected that imitation will be relatively free of resentment when it is possible for the imitators to identify themselves wholeheartedly with their model. It is the great misfortune of our time that in the present surge of Westernization so

---

[*] Islam came as such an agency, and its spread has been phenomenal in both Asia and Africa. Even at this moment it is still winning converts in the heart of Africa. One cannot help thinking that were the Moslem missionary to combine his religious preaching with technical know-how—link Islamization with industrialization—the spread of Islam might again become phenomenal.

many factors combine to keep the awakening countries from identifying themselves with the West they imitate. The fresh memory of colonialism, the color line, the difference in historical experience, the enormous gap in living standards, the fear of the educated minority in the backward countries that democracy and free enterprise would rob them of their birthright to direct, plan, and supervise—all these combine to create an attitude of suspicion and antagonism toward the West.

Less obvious is the fact that imitation is least impeded when we are made to feel that our act of imitation is actually an act of becoming the opposite of that which we imitate. A religion or civilization is most readily transmitted to alien societies by its heretical offspring which come into being as a protest and a challenge. Heresies have often served as vehicles for the transmission of ideas, attitudes, and ways of life. India influenced the Far East by a heresy it rejected (Buddhism), and Judaism impressed itself upon the world by a heresy it rejected (Christianity). Christianity itself, after it became the official religion of the Roman Empire, spread outside the core of the Graeco-Roman world mainly by its heresies. The Nestorians were Semites, the Jacobites Egyptians, and the Donatists Berbers. And if Communism is likely to become a vehicle for the transmission of Western achievement to non-Western countries it is due partly to the fact that Communism is a Western, and particularly a Capitalist, heresy which the West rejected.

Since I have called Communism a Capitalist heresy, it may not be out of place to consider here briefly the nature and genesis of heresies. A heresy can spring only from a system that is in full vigor. There is hardly an instance of a declining system giving birth to a heresy and being supplanted by it. At the birth of Christianity the militant spirit of Judaism was at a white heat, and Christianity was one of several Jewish heresies. Christianity itself was bursting with heresies during its youthful growth, and later during its militant ascendancy in the West. A time of great religious fervor is optimal for only for the rise of saints and martyrs but also for the pullulation of schisms and heresies. Where there is static orthodoxy or sheer indifference there is the least likelihood of fervent deviations and mutations. It is a measure of Capitalism's vigor that it could produce so forceful a heresy. To call Communism a Christian heresy, as Toynbee and others have done, is to shut one's eyes to the present state of Christianity and misread the true nature of Communism.

As I said, a heresy is a byproduct of exuberance and ebullience. It is by exaggerating, overfulfilling, and reaching out for extremes that a heresy breaks away from the parent body. There is apparently no surer way of turning a thing into its opposite than by exaggerating it. Professor Joseph Klausner said of Jesus that "by overfilling Judaism he caused his disciples to make of it non-Judaism"; and it is by "overfilling" Capitalism that the Communists make of it non-Capitalism. Ever since Capitalism came into its own we have caught glimpses of the Capitalists' dream of omnipotence. It is a dream of total noninterference—of a "company state" rather than a company within a state. Some Capitalists tried to realize this dream in distant colonies where they were unrestrained by the mores and traditions of their homeland. But only Communist regime succeeds in making the wildest Capitalist dream come true right in the home country. A monolithic company —the Communist party—takes possession of a whole country. It not only owns every acre of land, every building factory, etc., but has absolute dominion over the bodies and souls of every man, woman, and child. The aim of this super-Capitalist company is to turn the captive population into skilled mechanics and so shape their souls that they would toil from sunup to sundown, thankful to be alive and blessing their exploiters. It is only natural that such a "company state" should aspire to turn itself into a holding company of the whole planet.

Even when a Communist regime is wholly free of Stalinist viciousness it can still be seen as an attempt to overfulfill Capitalism.

22

In a Capitalist system, the productive process is hampered by the trivial motivation of the owner, the recalcitrance of the worker, and the capriciousness of the consumer. It needs a prodigious expenditure of energy and substance to counteract the vitiating effect of these factors. Communism, with one sweep, rids Capitalism of the anarchic owner, worker, and consumer. It makes of production an uncompromising deity which brooks no interference from any quarter.

Finally, Communism is repeating a pattern followed by other heresies when it strives to separate Capitalism from the Capitalists. The Christian heresy detached Judaism from the Jews, and the Protestant heresy separated Catholicism from the Catholic hierarchy. And remembering the battle cry of the Kronstadt uprising, it is permissible to predict that the slogan of an eventual Communist heresy will be: "Communism without Communists."

An awareness that rapid modernization is essentially a process of imitation helps us not only to make sense of the turmoil in the backward countries but also to gauge the durability of all that is being achieved there at present. When we see how wholly different the social and political conditions are in the underdeveloped countries from what they had been in Europe and America at the birth of the machine age, it is natural to wonder whether the transplantation of Western achievements to these countries is likely to be viable. However, when we keep in mind that what we are observing is an act of concerted imitation, the view changes completely. Conditions which are optimal for origination are not necessarily optimal for imitation. Origination requires a more or less loose social order in which the individual has leeway to tinker, follow his hunches and run risks on his own. On the other hand, rapid imitation is facilitated by social compactness, regimentation, and concerted action. The individual who is a member of a compact group is more imitative than the individual who is on his own. The unified individual is without a distinct self and, like the child, his mind is without guards against the intrusion of influences from without. The paradox is then that rapid modernization requires a primitivization of the social structure. The collectivist bias of the backward countries is thus likely to be an aid rather than a hindrance in their race to catch up with the West.

5 · The Readiness to Work

T
he other day I happened to ask myself a routine question and stumbled on a surprising answer. The question was: What is the uppermost problem which confronts the leadership in a Communist regime? The answer: The chief preoccupation of every government between the Elbe and the China Sea is how to make people work—how to induce them to plow, sow, harvest, build, manufacture, work in the mines, and so forth. It is the most vital problem which confronts them day in day out, and it shapes not only their domestic policies but their relations with the outside world.

One is struck by the strangeness of it: that a movement which set out to achieve a miraculous transformation of man and society should have succeeded in transforming into a miracle something which to us is entirely natural and matter-of-fact. In the Occident the chief problem is not how to induce people to work but how to find enough jobs for people who want to work. We seem to take the readiness to work almost as much for granted as the readiness to breathe. Yet the goings on inside the Communist world serve to remind us that the Occident's attitude toward work, so far from being natural and normal, is strange and unprecedented. It was the relatively recent emergence of this attitude which, as much as anything else, gave modern Western civilization its unique character and marked it off from all its predecessors.

In practically all civilizations we know of, and in the Occident too for many centuries, work was viewed as a curse, a mark of bondage, or, at best, a necessary evil. That free men should be willing to work day after day, even after their vital needs are satisfied, and that work should be seen as a mark of uprightness and manly worth, is not only unparalleled in history but remains more or less incomprehensible to many people outside the Occident.

The Occident's novel attitude toward work is traced by some to the rules of St. Benedict (circa A.D. 530) which prescribed manual labor (six hours a day in winter and seven hours in summer) for every monk in the Benedictine monasteries. Hereby the contemptuous attitude of the classical world toward work, as fit only for slaves, was turned into reverence. The new attitude penetrated into the towns which usually grew around the monasteries, and from there was diffused farther afield. Still, the fact remains that in the Middle Ages people did not show any marked inclination to work more than was necessary to maintain a fairly low standard of living. It was only in the sixteenth century that we see emerging a strange addiction to work.

According to Max Weber and others, it was Luther's idea of the sacredness of Man's calling, and particularly Calvin's doctrine of predestination, which infused a new seriousness into man's daily doings. According to Calvin salvation and eternal damnation are predestined from the foundation of the world. No one can know whether he is of the few predestined to everlasting life or of the many foreordained to everlasting death. But since it is natural to assume that the chosen would succeed in whatever they undertake while the damned would fail, one was spurred to strive with all one's might for worldly success as proof of one's salvation. Erich Fromm complements this theory by pointing out that the unbearable uncertainty induced by this doctrine would by itself drive people to "frantic activity and a striving to do something."

Still, it is highly doubtful whether the tremendous dynamism displayed by the Occident during the past four hundred years was fueled mainly by religious elements or derivatives. The decisive factor in the development of modern Western civilization was not the psychological effect of some religious idea or doctrine but the mass emergence of the autonomous individual. And it is plausible that the Reformation itself was a byproduct of the process of individualization.

We are not concerned here with the manner in which the individual was released from the compact corporate pattern of the Middle Ages. A fortuitous combination of circumstances, not the least of which was the spread of literacy by the introduction of paper and printing, brought about a cracking and crumbling of the feudal economy and a loosening of the grip of an all-embracing Catholic Church. Whether he willed it or not, the Western European individual, toward the end of the fifteenth century, found himself more or less on his own. Now the separation of the individual from a collective body, even when it is ardently striven for, is a painful experience. The newly emerging individual is an unstable and explosive entity. This is true of the young who cut loose from the family and venture forth on their own; of persons who break away or are separated from a compact tribe, clan, community, party, or clique; of discharged soldiers separated from the corporate life of an army; and even of freed slaves removed from the intimate corporate life of slave quarters. An autonomous existence is heavily burdened and beset with fears, and can be endured only when bolstered by confidence and self-esteem. The individual's most vital need is to prove his worth, and this usually means an insatiable hunger for action. For it is only the few who can acquire a sense of worth by developing and employing their capacities and talents. The majority prove their worth by keeping busy. A busy life is the nearest thing to a purposeful life. But whether the individual takes the path of self-realization or the easier one of self-justification by action he remains unbalanced and restless. For he has to prove his worth anew each day. It does not require the uncertainties of an outlandish doctrine of predestination to drive him to "frantic effort and a striving to do something."

The burst of activity and creativeness we know as the Renaissance was in full swing before Luther and Calvin entered the field. It was the individualization of a once corporate society which manifested itself as an awakening and a renascence. The Reformation itself was a byproduct of this individualization—a reaction against it. For there are many who find the burdens, the anxiety, and the isolation of an individual existence unbearable. This is particularly true when the opportunities for self-advancement are relatively meager, and one's individual interests and prospects do not seem worth living for. Such persons sooner or later turn their backs on an individual existence and strive to acquire a sense of worth and of purpose by an identification with a holy cause, a leader, or a movement. The faith and pride they derive from such an identification serve them as substitutes for the unattainable self-confidence and self-respect. The movement of the Reformation was to begin with such an escape from the burden of an autonomous existence.

Luther and Calvin did not come to liberate the individual from the control of an authoritarian church. "The Reformation," says Max Weber, "meant not the elimination of the church's control over everyday life, but rather the substitution of a new form of control for the previous one. It meant the repudiation of a control which was very lax, at that time barely perceptible in practice, and hardly more than formal, in favor of a regulation of the whole conduct which, penetrating to all departments of private and public life, was infinitely burdensome and earnestly enforced." * The rule of Calvinism as enforced in Geneva and elsewhere was inimical to individual autonomy not only in religious matters but in all departments of life. Had Luther and Calvin had at their disposal the fearful instruments of coercion of a Hitler or a Stalin, they would have perhaps herded back the emerging individual into the communal corral, and would have stifled the new Occident at its birth. As it was, the European individual mastered the Reformation and

---

* Max Weber, *The Protestant Ethic and the Spirit of Capitalism* (London: G. Allen & Unwin, 1930), pp. 36-37

used it for his own ends. He used faith to lubricate his machine of action and legitimize his success. He rushed headlong into the thousand new paths to action and fortune opened by the discovery of new continents and trade routes and the development of new sciences and techniques. He reached out to the four corners of the earth, carrying his restlessness with him and infecting the whole world with it.

To an outside observer, an individualist society seems in the grip of some strange obsession. Its ceaseless agitation strikes him as a kind of madness. And, indeed, action is basically a reaction against loss of balance—a flailing of the arms to regain one's balance. To dispose a soul to action, we must upset its equilibrium. And if, as Napoleon wrote to Carnot, "the art of government is not to let men go stale," then it is essentially an art of unbalancing. This is particularly true in an industrialized society which requires a population disposed to continued exertion and alertness. The crucial difference between the Communist regimes and the individualist Occident is thus perhaps in the methods of unbalancing by which their masses are kept active and striving.

The Communists started out as miracle workers. Not only were they to bring about a miraculous transformation of man and society but the material tasks, too, which they set themselves—the industrialization and modernization of vast territories—were to partake of the miraculous. These tasks were to be realized by the energies released by a creed, and they were to demonstrate the validity and superiority of this creed. To proceed soberly, after a careful mobilization of skill, equipment, and material, would be to act in the manner of men of little faith. One had to plunge headlong into one grandiose project after another, heedless of the waste and suffering involved. Faith, dedication, and self-sacrifice were to accomplish the impossible.

Much has been said by all manner of people in praise of enthusiasm. The important point is that enthusiasm is ephemeral, and hence unserviceable for the long haul. One can hardly conceive of a more unhealthy and wasteful state of affairs than where faith and dedication are requisite for the performance of unmiraculous everyday activities. The attempt to keep people enthusiastic once they have ceased to believe is productive of the most pernicious consequences. An enormous effort has to be expended to maintain the revivalist spirit and, inevitably, with the passage of time, the fuels used to generate enthusiasm become more crude and poisonous. The Communists started out with faith and extravagant hope, then passed to pride and hatred, and finally settled on fear. The use of terror to evoke enthusiasm was one of Stalin's most pernicious inventions. For he did succeed in extracting strength from crushed souls.

The Communists did not withhold their hand from other modes of unbalancing. The transportation of vast populations from one end of the land to another; the shifting of muzhiks to towns and of townspeople to farms; the periodic purges; the sudden changes in the party line—such were some of the crude jolts by which they tried to keep the masses from going stale.

There is no doubt that the Communists can point to tremendous industrial achievements during the past forty years. But even while Stalin was alive, it must have dawned on some of the leaders that the techniques of generating enthusiasm, despite their impressive potentialities, cannot achieve the smooth effortlessness which is the outstanding characteristic of a genuine machine age. If in order to keep the wheels turning you have to deafen ears with propaganda, crack the whip of Terror, and keep pushing people around, then you haven't got a machine civilization no matter how numerous and ingenious your machines.

In an individualist society, the mode of unbalancing is far more subtle, and requires relatively little prompting from without. For the autonomous individual constitutes a chronically unbalanced entity. The confidence and sense of worth which alone can keep him on an even keel are extremely perishable and must be generated anew each day. An achievement today is but a challenge for tomorrow. And since it is mainly by work that the majority of individuals prove their worth and regain their balance, they must keep at it continuously. Hence the ceaseless hustling of an individualist society.

No one will claim that the majority of people in the Western world, be they workers or managers, find fulfillment in their work. But they do find in it a justification of their existence. The ability to do a day's work and get paid for it gives one a sense of usefulness and worth. The paycheck and the profitable balance sheet are certificates of value. Where the job requires exceptional skill or tests a person's capacities there is an additional sense of exhilaration. But even a job of the sheerest routine yields the individual something besides the wherewithal of a living.

The significance of a job in the life of the Occidental individual is made particularly clear by the state of mind of the unemployed. There is little doubt that the frustration engendered by unemployment is due more to a corrosive sense of worthlessness than to economic hardship. Unemployment pay, however adequate, cannot mitigate it. In the Occident it is inaction rather than actual hardship which breeds discontent and disaffection. In America even the legitimate retirement after a lifetime of work constitutes a fearsome crisis. In the longshoremen's union in San Francisco, the award of a $200-a-month pension to men over sixty-five, who had twenty-five years of service on the waterfront, brought in its wake a sudden rise in the rate of death among the retired. It is now recognized that men must be conditioned for retirement so as to endow them with a specific kind of endurance. Herbert Hoover on his eighty-second birthday echoed a widespread feeling when he said that a man who retires from work "shrivels up into a nuisance to all mankind."

It is to be expected that where a sense of worth is attainable without effort, when one is born with it so to speak, the readiness to work is not likely to be pronounced. Thus in societies where the Negro race is officially designated as inferior, and every white person can feel himself a member of a superior race, the pressure of individual self-assertion by work is considerably reduced. The presence of indolent "white trash" is usually a characteristic of such societies. A somewhat similar situation is to be observed in class- or caste-bound societies.

The remarkable thing is that the Occident's addiction to work is by no means synonymous with a love of work. The Western workingman actually has the illusion that he can kill work and be done with it. He "attacks" every job he undertakes and feels the ending of a task as a victory. Those who, like the Negro, know that work is eternal tend to take it easy.

The individualist society which manifests a marked readiness to work is one in which individualism is widely diffused. It is the individual in the mass who turns to work as a means of proving his worth and usefulness. Things are different where individualism is exclusive, as it was in Greece. The exclusive individual will tend to prove his worth and usefulness by managing and leading others or by developing and exercising his capacities and talents. Work, though it be hard and unceasing, is actually an easy solution of the problems which confront the autonomous individual, and it is not surprising that the individual in the mass should take this easy way out.

It hardly needs emphasizing that the individualist society we are talking about is not one in which every individual is unique—with judgments, tastes, and attitudes distinctly his own. All that one can claim for the individual in such a society is that he is more or less on his own; that he chooses his course through life, proves himself by his own efforts, and has to shoulder the responsibility for what he makes of his life. It is obvious, therefore, that it is individual freedom which generates the readiness to work. On the face of it, this is rather startling. It means that when the mass of people are free to work or not to work they usually act as if they are driven to work. Freedom releases the energies of the masses not by exhilarating but by unbalancing, irritating, and goading. You do not go to a free society to find carefree people. When we leave people on their own, we are delivering them into the hands of a ruthless taskmaster from whose bondage there is no escape. The individual who has to justify his existence by his own efforts is in eternal bondage to himself.

There is a remarkable statement made in 1958 by the director of industry and commerce in the Indian state of Andhra Pradesh. "It is harder," he said, "to provide the members of a community with shelter, clothing, and food than to launch an artificial satellite." The words sound odd in our ears, but they underline a now familiar paradox: the revolutionary governments which have sprung up in recent decades in all parts of the world see themselves as the embodiment of the popular will, yet they do not know how to make the masses work. They know how to generate popular enthusiasm and how to induce in the masses a readiness to fight, but they seem helpless in anything which requires an automatic readiness on the part of the masses to work day in day out. On the other hand, the same governments do not find it hard to create conditions favorable for the performance of scientists, professors, top technicians, and intellectuals in general. They know how to foster the exceptional skills requisite for the manufacture of complex machinery and instruments, even the harnessing of the atom and launching of satellites.

There is little likelihood that the intellectuals who constitute the leading element in these new governments would be receptive to the idea that, in the case of the masses, there is a connection between individual freedom and the readiness to work; that individual freedom is a potent factor in energizing and activating the masses. To an intelligentsia preoccupied with planning, managing, and guiding, no idea will seem so patently absurd as that the masses, if left wholly to themselves, would labor and strive of their own accord.

The interesting thing is that the energizing effect of freedom seems confined to the masses. There is no unequivocal evidence that the intellectual is at his creative best when left wholly on his own. It is not at all certain that individual freedom is a vital factor in the release of creative energies in literature, art, music, and science. Many of the outstanding achievements in these fields were not realized in an atmosphere of absolute freedom. Certainly in this country cultural creativeness has not been proportionate to our degree of individual freedom. There is a chronic insecurity at the core of the creative person, and he needs a milieu that will nourish his confidence and sense of uniqueness. Discerning appreciation and a modicum of deference and acclaim are probably more vital for his creative flow than freedom to fend for himself. Thus a despotism that recognizes and subsidizes excellence might be more favorable for the performance of the intellectual than a free society that does not take him seriously. Coleridge protested that "the darkest despotisms on the continent have done more for the growth and elevation of the fine arts than the English government. A great musical composer in Germany and Italy is a great man in society and a real dignity and rank are conceded him. So it is with the sculptor or painter or architect. ... In this country there is no general reverence for the fine arts." It is of course conceivable that a wholly free society might become imbued with a reverence for the fine arts; but up to now the indications have been that where common folk have room enough there is not much room for the dignity and rank of the typical writer, artist, and intellectual in general.

The paradox is, then, that although the intellectual has been in the forefront of the struggle for individual freedom, he can never feel wholly at home in a free society. He finds there neither an unquestioned sense of usefulness nor favorable conditions for the realization of his talents. Hence the contradiction between what the intellectual professes while he battles the status quo, and what he practices once he comes to power. At present, in every part of the world, we see how revolutionary movements initiated by idealistic intellectuals and preserved in their keeping tend to crystallize into hierarchical social orders in which an aristocratic intelligentsia commands and the masses are expected to obey. Such social orders, as we have seen, are ideal for the performance of the intellectual but not for that of the masses. It is this circumstance rather than the corruption of power which has been turning idealistic intellectuals into strident, ruthless slavedrivers.

The vital question is of course whether the masses, energized and activated by freedom, can create aught worthwhile on their own. Though the masses have been with us from the beginning of time, we know little about their creative potentialities. In all the fifty centuries of history, the masses had apparently only one chance to show what they could do on their own, without masters to push them around, and it needed the discovery of a new world to give them that chance. In his Last Essays, Georges Bernanos remarks that the French empire was not an achievement of the masses but of a small band of heroes. It is equally true that the masses did not make the British, German, Russian, Chinese, or Japanese empires. But the masses made America. They were the vanguard: they infiltrated, shoved, stole, fought, incorporated, founded, and raised the flag—

And all the disavouched, hard-bitten pack
Shipped overseas to steal a continent
With neither shirts nor honor to their back. [*]

It is this fact which gives America its utter newness. All civilizations we know of were shaped by exclusive minorities of kings,

---

[*] Stephen Vincent Benet, *John Brown's Body* (New York: Doubleday, Doran & Company, 1928).

nobles, priests, and the equivalents of the intellectual. It was they who formulated the ideals, aspirations, and values, and it was they who set the tone. America is the only instance of a civilization shaped and colored by the tastes and values of common folk. No elite of whatever nature can feel truly at home in America. This is true not only of the aristocrat proper, but also of the intellectual, the military leader, the business tycoon, and even the labor leader.

The deprecators of America usually point to its defects as being those of a business civilization. Actually they are the defects of the mass: worship of success, the cult of the practical, the identification of quality with quantity, the addiction to sheer action, the fascination with the trivial. We also know the virtues: a superb dynamism, an unprecedented diffusion of skills, a genius for organization and teamwork, a flexibility which makes possible an easy adjustment to the most drastic change, an ability to get things done with a minimum of tutelage and supervision, an unbounded capacity for fraternization.

So much for the defects and the virtues. What of the creative potentialities? My feeling has always been that the people I work and live with are lumpy with talents. We do not know enough of the nature of the creative process to maintain that a sense of uniqueness is crucial to the creative flow. Certainly, the American's wariness of people with a claim to uniqueness is not synonymous with an aversion to excellence. The American perfects and polishes his way of doing things, whether in work or in play, the way the French of the seventeenth century polished their maxims and aphorisms. The realization of the creative potentialities of the masses hinges on the possibility of a diffusion of expertise in literature, art, music, and science comparable with the existing wide diffusion of expertise in mechanics and sports.

We know of one instance in the past where the masses entered the field of cultural creativeness not as mere onlookers but as participators. We are told that Florence at the time of the Renaissance had more artists than citizens. Where did these artists come from?

Craftsmen and their workshops played a vital role in the unfolding of the new painting and sculpture. The Renaissance was born in the marketplace. Almost all the great artists were apprenticed when children to craftsmen. They were mostly the sons of artisans, shopkeepers, peasants, and petty officials. The sixteenth-century historian Benedetto Varchi says of the Florentines: "I have always been very much surprised to see that in these men who have been accustomed from childhood to carry heavy bales of wool and baskets of silk and who spend all day and a large part of the night glued to their looms and spindles there should dwell so great a spirit and such high and noble thoughts." Everyday life was permeated by an interest in the procedures and techniques of the arts. One can hardly imagine a Florentine painter of that time making the remark, attributed to Marcel Duchamp, that "when painting becomes so low that laymen talk about it, it doesn't interest me." Even the greatest of the Florentine painters and sculptors had an intimate contact with everyday life, and lacked the disdain of the practical characteristic of the artists of ancient Greece and of our time. Verocchio, Alberti, and Leonardo da Vinci had a passionate interest in practical devices, machines, and gadgets. They were no more fastidious and no less "materialistic" than artisans and merchants. There is no evidence that cultural creativeness is incompatible with relatively gross bents, drives, and incentives.

Though it may be questioned whether the lesson of Florence is applicable to a country of millions, it does suggest that the businesslike atmosphere of the workshop is more favorable for the awakening and unfolding of the creative talents of the masses than the precious atmosphere of artistic cliques. As we shall see, the increase in leisure due to the spread of automation makes the participation of the masses in cultural creativeness an element of social health and stability. Such a participation seems more feasible when we think of turning the masses into creative craftsmen rather than into artists and literati.

6 · The Intellectual and the Masses

The intellectual as a champion of the masses is a relatively recent phenomenon. Education does not naturally waken in us a concern for the uneducated. The distinction conferred by education is more easily maintained by a sharp separation from those below than by a continued excellence of achievement. When Gandhi was asked by an American clergyman what it was that worried him most, he replied: "The hardness of heart of the educated."

In almost every civilization we know of, the intellectuals have been either allied with those in power or members of a governing elite, and consequently indifferent to the fate of the masses. In ancient Egypt and Imperial China, the literati were magistrates, overseers, stewards, tax-gatherers, secretaries, and officials of every kind. They were in command and did not lift a finger to lighten the burden of the lower orders. In India the intellectuals were members of the uppermost caste of the Brahmins. Gautama, who preached love of service for others and the mixing of castes, was by birth not an intellectual but a warrior; and the attempt to translate Buddha's teaching into reality was made by another warrior—Emperor Asoka. The Brahmin intellectuals, far from rallying to the cause, led the opposition to Buddhism, and finally drove it out of India. In classical Greece, the intellectuals were at the top of the social ladder: philosophers and poets were also legislators, generals, and statesmen. This intellectual elite had an ingrained contempt for the common people who did the world's work, regarding them as no better than slaves and unfit for citizenship. In the Roman Empire, the intellectuals, whether Greek or Roman, made common cause with the powers that be, and kept their distance from the masses. In medieval Europe, too, the intellectual was a member of a privileged order—the Church—and did not manifest undue solicitude for the underprivileged.

In only one society prior to the emergence of the modern Occident, do we find a group of "men of words" raising their voices in defense of the weak and oppressed. For many centuries the small nation of the ancient Hebrews on the eastern shore of the Mediterranean did not differ markedly in its institutions and spiritual life from its neighbors. But in the eighth century B.C., owing to an obscure combination of circumstances, it began to develop a most strange deviation. Side by side with the traditional men of words—priests, counselors, soothsayers, scribes—there emerged a series of extraordinary men who pitted themselves against the ruling elite and the prevailing social order. These men, the prophets, were in many ways the prototype of the modern militant intellectual. Renan speaks of them as "open-air journalists" who recited their articles in the street and marketplace, and at the city gate. "The first article of irreconcilable journalism was written by Amos about 800 B.C." Many of the characteristic attitudes of the modern intellectual—his tendency to see any group he identifies himself with as a chosen people, and any truth he embraces as the one and only truth; the envisioning of a millennial society on earth—are clearly discerned in the prophets. The ideals, also, and the holy causes that the intellectuals are preaching and propagating today were fully formulated during the three centuries in which the prophets were active.

We know too little about these remote centuries to explain the rise of the prophets. The temptation is great to look for circumstances not unlike those which attended the rise of the militant men of words in the modern Occident. One wonders whether a diffusion of literacy in the ninth century B.C. was not one of the factors. It was at about that time that the Phoenician traders perfected the simple alphabet from the complex and cumbersome picture writing of the Egyptians. And considering the close relations which prevailed then between Phoenicians and Hebrews, it would not be unreasonable to assume that the latter were quick to adopt the new easy writing. Particularly during the reign of Solomon (960-925 B.C.) the intimate link with Phoenicia and the need for an army of scribes to run Solomon's centralized and bureaucratized admini-stration must have resulted in a sharp rise in the number of literate Hebrews. Such an increase in literacy was fraught with conse-quences for Hebrew society. In Phoenicia the new alphabet was primarily an instrument of commerce, and the sudden increase in the number of literate persons presented no problem, for they were rapidly absorbed in the far-flung trade organizations. But the chiefly agricultural Hebrew society was swamped by a horde of unemployed scribes when the bureaucratic apparatus crumbled at Solomon's death. The new unattached scribes found themselves suspended between the privileged clique, whose monopoly on reading and writing they had broken, and the illiterate masses, to whom they were allied by birth. Since they had neither position nor adequate employment, it was natural that they should align themselves against established privilege, and become self-appoint-ed spokesmen of their inarticulate brethren. Such at least might have been the circumstances at the rise of the earliest prophets—of Amos the shepherd of Tekoa and his disciples. They set the pattern, and the road trodden by them was later followed by men of all walks of life, even by Isaiah the aristocrat.

The rise of the militant intellectual in the Occident was brought about not by a simplification of the art of writing but by the introduction of paper and printing. Undoubtedly the Church's monopoly of education was considerably weakened, as I have said, in the late Middle Ages. But it was the introduction of paper and printing that finished the job. The new men of words, like those of the eighth century B.C., were on the whole unattached allied with neither Church nor government. They had no clear status, and no self-evident role of social usefulness. In the social orders evolved by the modern Occident, power and influence were, and to a large extent still are, in the hands of industrialists, businessmen, bankers, landowners, and soldiers. The intellectual feels himself on the outside. Even when he is widely acclaimed and highly rewarded, he does not feel himself part of the ruling elite. He finds himself almost superfluous in a civilization which is largely his handiwork. Small wonder that he tends to resent those in power as intruders and usurpers.

Thus the antagonism between men of words and men of action which first emerged as a historical motif among the Hebrews in the eighth century B.C., and made of them a peculiar people, reappeared in the sixteenth century in the life of the modern Occident and set it apart from all other civilizations. The unattached intellectual's unceasing search for a recognized status and a useful role has brought him to the forefront of every movement of change since the Reformation, not only in the West but wherever Western influence has penetrated. He has consistently sought a link with the underprivileged, be they bourgeois, peasants, proletarians, persecuted minorities, or the natives of colonial countries. So far, his most potent alliance has been with the masses.

The coming together of the intellectual and the masses has proved itself a formidable combination, and there is no doubt that it was largely instrumental in bringing about the unprecedented advancement of the masses in modern times. Yet, despite its achievements, the combination is not based on a real affinity.

The intellectual goes to the masses in search of weightiness and a role of leadership. Unlike the man of action, the man of words needs the sanction of ideals and the incantation of words in order to act forcefully. He wants to lead, command, and conquer, but he must feel that in satisfying these hungers he does not cater to a petty self. He needs justification, and he seeks it in the realization of a grandiose design, and in the solemn ritual of making the word become flesh. Thus he does battle for the downtrodden and disinherited, and for liberty, equality, justice, and truth, though, as Thoreau pointed out, the grievance which animates him is not mainly "his sympathy with his fellows in distress, but, though he be the holiest son of God, is his private ail." Once his "private ail" is righted, the intellectual's ardor for the underprivileged cools considerably. His cast of mind is essentially aristocratic. Like Heraclitus he is convinced that "ten thousand [of the masses] do not turn the scale against a single man of worth" and that "the many are mean; only the few are noble." He sees himself as a leader and master.* Not only does he doubt that the masses could do anything worthwhile on their own, but he would resent it if they made the attempt. The masses must obey. They need the shaping force of discipline in both war and peace. It is indeed doubtful that the typical intellectual would feel wholly at home in a society where the masses got their share of the fleshpots. Not only would there be little chance for leadership where people were almost without a grievance, but we might suspect that the cockiness and the airs of an affluent populace would offend his aristocratic sensibilities.

There is considerable evidence that when the militant intellectual succeeds in establishing a social order in which his craving for a superior status and social usefulness is fully satisfied, his view of the masses darkens, and from being their champion he becomes their detractor. The struggle initiated by the prophets in the eighth century B.C. ended, some three hundred years later, in the complete victory of the men of words. After the return from the

---

* In 1935 a group of students at Rangoon University banded themselves together into a revolutionary group and immediately added the prefix "Thakin" (master) to their names.

Babylonian captivity, the scribes and the scholars were supreme and the Hebrew nation became "a people of the book." Once dominant, these scribes, like the Pharisees who succeeded them, flaunted their loathing for the masses. They made of the word for common folk, "am-ha-aretz," a term of derision and scorn—even the gentle Hillel taught that "no am-ha-aretz can be pious." Yet these scribes had an unassailable hold on the masses they despised. The noble carpenter from Galilee could make no headway when he challenged the pretension of the solemn scholars, hair-splitting lawyers, and arrogant pedants, and raised his voice in defense of the poor in spirit. He was ostracized and anathematized, and his teachings found a following chiefly among non-Jews. Yet the teachings of Jesus fared no better than the teachings of the prophets when they came wholly into the keeping of dominant intellectuals. They were made into a vehicle for the maintenance and aggrandizement of a vast hierarchy of clerks, while the poor in spirit, instead of inheriting the earth, were left to sink into serfdom and superstitious darkness.

In the sixteenth century, we see the same pattern again. When Luther first defied the Pope and his councils he spoke feelingly of "the poor, simple, common folk." Later, when allied with the German princelings, he lashed out against the rebellious masses with unmatched ferocity: "Let there be no half-measures! Cut their throats! Transfix them! Leave no stone unturned! To kill a rebel is to destroy a mad dog." He assured his aristocratic patrons that "a prince can enter heaven by the shedding of blood more certainly than others by means of prayer."

It is the twentieth century, however, which has given us the most striking example of the discrepancy between the attitude of the intellectual while the struggle is on, and his role once the battle is won. Marxism started out as a movement for the salvation of both the masses and the intellectuals from the degradation and servitude of a capitalist social order. The *Communist Manifesto* condemned the bourgeoisie not only for pauperizing, dehumani-

zing, and enslaving the toiling masses, but also for robbing the
intellectual of his elevated status. "The bourgeoisie has stripped of
its halo every occupation hitherto honored and looked up to with
reverent awe." Though the movement was initiated by intellectuals
and powered by their talents and hungers, it yet held up the prole-
tariat as the chosen people—the only carrier of the revolutionary
idea, and the chief beneficiary of the revolution to come. The
intellectuals, particularly those who had "raised themselves to the
level of comprehending theoretically the historical movement as a
whole," were to act as guides—as a composite Moses—during the
long wanderings in the desert. Like Moses, the intellectuals would
have no more to do once the promised land was in sight. "The role
of the intelligentsia," said Lenin, "is to make special leaders from
among the intelligentsia unnecessary."

The Marxist movement has made giant strides during the past
forty years. It has created powerful political parties in many
countries, and it is in possession of absolute power in the vast
stretch of land between the Elbe and the China Sea. In Russia,
China, and adjacent smaller countries, the revolution envisaged by
Marxism has been consummated. What, then, is the condition of
the masses and the intellectuals in these countries?

In no other social order, past or present, has the intellectual so
completely come into his own as in the Communist regimes. Never
before has his superior status been so self-evident and his social
usefulness so unquestioned. The bureaucracy which manages and
controls every field of activity is staffed by people who consider
themselves intellectuals. Writers, poets, artists, scientists, professors, journalists, and others engaged in intellectual pursuits are
accorded the high social status of superior civil servants. They are
the aristocrats, the rich, the prominent, the indispensable, the
pampered and petted. It is the wildest dream of the man of words
come true.

And what of the masses in this intellectual's paradise? They
have found in the intellectual the most formidable taskmaster in

history. No other regime has treated the masses so callously as raw material, to be experimented on and manipulated at will; and never before have so many lives been wasted so recklessly in war and in peace. On top of all this, the Communist intelligentsia has been using force in a wholly novel manner. The traditional master uses force to exact obedience and lets it go at that. Not so the intellectual. Because of his professed faith in the power of words and the irresistibility of the truths which supposedly shape his course, he cannot be satisfied with mere obedience. He tries to obtain by force a response that is usually obtained by the most perfect persuasion, and he uses Terror as a fearful instrument to extract faith and fervor from crushed souls.

One cannot escape the impression that the intellectual's most fundamental incompatibility is with the masses. He has managed to thrive in social orders dominated by kings, nobles, priests, and merchants, but not in societies suffused with the tastes and values of the masses. The trespassing by the masses into the domain of culture and onto the stage of history is seen even by the best among the intellectuals as a calamity. Heine viewed with horror the mass society taking shape on the North American continent— "that monstrous prison of freedom where the invisible chains would oppress me even more than the visible ones at home, and where the most repulsive of tyrants, the populace, holds vulgar sway." Nietzsche feared that the invasion of the masses would turn history into a shallow swamp. The masses, says Karl Jaspers, exert "an immense gravitational pull which seems again and again to paralyze every upward sweep. The tremendous forces of the masses, with their attributes of mediocrity suffocate whatever is not in line with them." To Emerson, the masses were "rude, lame, unmade, pernicious in their demands and influence, and need not to be flattered but to be schooled. I wish not to concede anything to

45

them, but to tame, drill, divide and break them up, and draw individuals out of them. ... If government knew how, I should like to see it check, not multiply, the population." Flaubert saw no hope in the masses: they "never come of age, and will always be at the bottom of the social scale. ..." He thought it of little importance "that many peasants should be able to read and no longer heed their priests; but it is infinitely important that men like Renan and Littré should be able to live and be listened to."

Renan himself, so wise and humane, could not hold back his loathing for the masses. He thought that popular education, so far from making the masses wiser, "only destroys their natural amiability, their instincts, their innate sound reason, and renders them positively unendurable." After the debacle of 1870, Renan spent several months in seclusion writing his *Philosophical Dialogues*, in which he vented his spleen not on the political and cultural elite which was responsible for France's defeat, but on democracy and the masses. The principle that society exists for the well-being of the mass of people does not seem to him consistent with the plan of nature. "It is much to be feared that the last expression of democracy may be a social state with a degenerate populace having no other aim than to indulge in the ignoble appetites of the vulgar." The purpose of an ideal social order is less to produce enlightened masses than uncommon people. "If the ignorance of the masses is a necessary condition for this end, so much the worse for the masses." He is convinced that a high culture is hardly to be imagined without the full subordination of the masses, and he envisages a world ruled by an elite of wise men possessed of absolute power and capable of striking terror into the hearts of the vulgar. This dictatorship of the wise would have hell at its command; "not a chimerical hell of whose existence there is no proof, but a veritable hell." It would institute a preventive Terror, not unlike that instituted by Stalin sixty years later, "with a view to frighten people and prevent their defending themselves," and it would "hardly hesitate to maintain in some lost district in Asia a nucleus of Bashkirs and Kalmuks, obedient machines, unencumbered by moral scruples and prepared for every sort of cruelty."

It is remarkable how closely the attitude of the intellectual toward the masses resembles the attitude of a colonial functionary toward the natives. The intellectual groaning under the dead weight of the inert masses reminds us of sahibs groaning under the white man's burden. Small wonder that when we observe a regime by intellectuals in action, whether in Russia or in Portugal, we have the feeling that here colonialism begins at home. Nor should it be surprising that liberation movements in the colonies spearheaded by intellectuals result in a passage from colonialism by Whites to colonialism by Blacks.

In the essay on "The Readiness to Work" it has been suggested that the masses are not likely to perform well in a social order shaped and run by intellectuals. Some measure of coercion, even of enslavement, is apparently needed to keep the masses working in such a regime. However, with the coming of automation, it may eventually be possible for a ruling intelligentsia to operate a country's economy without the aid of the masses, and it is legitimate to speculate on what the intellectual may be tempted to do with the masses once they become superfluous. Dostoyevsky, with his apocalyptic premonition of things to come, puts the following words in the mouth of an intellectual by the name of Lyamshin: "For my part, if I didn't know what to do with nine-tenths of mankind, I'd take them and blow them up into the air instead of putting them in paradise. I'd only leave a handful of educated people, who would live happily ever afterwards on scientific principles." * Now, it is highly unlikely that even the most ruthless intelligentsia would follow Lyamshin's recommenddation, though one has the feeling that Mao Tsetung's unconcern about a nuclear holocaust is perhaps bolstered by the wish to rid

---

* *The Possessed*, Modern Library edition (New York: Random House. 1936), p. 411.

his system of millions of superfluous Chinese. There is no reason, however, why a doctrine should not be propounded eventually that the masses are a poisonous waste product that must be kept under a tight lid and set apart as a caste of untouchables. That such a doctrine would not be alien to the mentality of the Communist intellectual is evident from pronouncements made by Communist spokesmen in East Germany after the rising of 1953. They maintained that the rebellious workers, though they looked and behaved like workers, were not the working class known by Marx, but a decadent mixture of unregenerate remnants of eliminated classes and types. The real workers, they said, were now in positions of responsibility and power. Bertolt Brecht suggested in an ironical vein that since the Communist government has lost confidence in the people, the simple thing to do is to dissolve the people and elect another.

Actually, the intellectual's dependence on the masses is not confined to the economic field. It goes much deeper. He has a vital need for the flow of veneration and worship that can come only from a vast, formless, inarticulate multitude. After all, God himself could have gotten along without men, yet He created them, to be adored, worshiped, and beseeched by them. What elation could the intellectual derive from dominating an aggregation of quarrelsome, backbiting fellow intellectuals? It is, moreover, the faith of the masses which nourishes and invigorates his own faith, Hermann Rauschning quotes a Nazi intellectual: "If I am disheartened and despairing, if I am deadbeat through the eternal party quarrels, and I go to a meeting and speak to these simple goodhearted, honest people, then I am refreshed again; then all my doubts leave me."

To sum up: The intellectual's concern for the masses is as a rule a symptom of his uncertain status and his lack of an unquestionable sense of social usefulness. It is the activities of the chronically thwarted intellectual which make it possible for the masses to get their share of the good things of life. When the intellectual comes into his own, he becomes a pillar of stability and finds all kinds of lofty reasons for siding with the strong against the weak.

It is, then, in the interest of the masses that the struggle between the intellectual and the prevailing dispensation should remain undecided. But can we justify a continuing state of affairs in which the most gifted part of the population is ever denied its heart's desire, while the masses go on from strength to strength?

Actually, an antagonism between the intellectual and the powers that be serves a more vital purpose than the advancement of the masses: it keeps the social order from stagnating. For the evidence seems clear that a society in which the educated are closely allied with the governing class is capable of a brilliant beginning but not of continued growth and development. Such a society often attains heights of excellence early in its career and then stops. Its history is in the main a record of stagnation and decline. This was true of the ancient river-valley civilizations in Egypt, Mesopotamia, and China, and of the younger civilizations in India, Persia, the Graeco-Roman world, Byzantium, and the world of Islam. We also see that the first step in the awakening of a stagnant society is the estrangement of the educated minority from the prevailing dispensation, which is usually effected by the penetration of some foreign influence. This change in the relations between the educated and the governing class has been a factor in almost every renascence, including that of Europe from the stagnation of the Middle Ages.

The creativeness of the intellectual is often a function of a thwarted craving for purposeful action and a privileged rank. It has its origin in the soul intensity generated in front of an insurmountable obstacle on the path to action. The genuine writer, artist, and even scientist are dissatisfied persons—as dissatisfied as the revolutionary—but are endowed with a capacity for transmuting their dissatisfaction into a creative impulse. A busy, purposeful life of action not only diverts energies from creative channels, but above all reduces the potent irritation which releases the secretion of creativity.

There is also the remarkable fact that where the intellectuals are in full charge they do not usually create a milieu conducive to genuine creativeness. The reason for this is to be found in the role of the noncreative pseudo-intellectual in such a system. The genuinely creative person lacks, as a rule, the temperament requisite for the seizure, the exercise, and, above all, the retention of power. Hence, when the intellectuals come into their own, it is usually the pseudo-intellectual who rules the roost, and he is likely to imprint his mediocrity and meagerness on every phase of cultural activity. Moreover, his creative impotence brews in him a murderous hatred of intellectual brilliance and he may be tempted, as Stalin was, to enforce a crude leveling of all intellectual activity.

Thus it can be seen that the chronic thwarting of the intellectual's craving for power serves a higher purpose than the wellbeing of common folk. The advancement of the masses is a mere byproduct of the uniquely human fact that discontent is at the root of the creative process: that the most gifted members of the human species are at their creative best when they cannot have their way, and must compensate for what they miss by realizing and cultivating their capacities and talents.

7 · The Practical Sense

Nowadays we take the practical attitude for granted. We seem to think that there is in most people an inborn inclination to make use of every device and circumstance to facilitate their work and further their ends. Yet it needs but a moment's reflection to realize that, so far from being natural, the practical sense has been throughout history a rare phenomenon. Its prevalence is a peculiarity of the Occident, and here, too, it has asserted itself only during the last two hundred years.

There was a period of superb practicalness in the Near East during the Late Neolithic Age (4000-3000 B.C.). It saw the harnessing of oxen and asses; the invention of the plow, wheeled cart, sailboat, calendar, and script; the discovery of metallurgy, artificial irrigation, brickmaking, fermentation, and other fundamental techniques and devices. One has the impression that the coming of civilization about 3000 B.C. tapered off a brilliant practical era.

From their first appearance, civilizations almost everywhere were preoccupied with the spectacular, the fantastic, the sublime, the absurd, and the playful—with hardly a trickle of ingenuity seeping into the practical and useful. The prehistoric discoveries and inventions remained the basis of everyday life in most countries down to our time. Technologically, the Neolithic Age lasted even in Western Europe down to the end of the eighteenth century. In Europe as late as the seventeenth century the view still prevailed that there was something preposterous and unseemly in using sublime knowledge for practical ends. We are told that when the mechanical inventor Salomon de Caus tried to interest Richelieu in the possibility of a jet engine he was locked up as a madman in an asylum. People who came forward with practical plans for increasing output by the use of more powerful and efficient machines were considered queer. It was only in the late seventeenth and early eighteenth centuries that some sort of liaison began to be established between "sublime" knowledge and practical application. Fontenelle eulogized the military engineer Vauban for bringing down mathematics from the skies and attaching it "to various kinds of mundane utility." On the eve of the Revolution, the French government was welcoming proposals for increasing output even when they were advanced by obvious cranks.

The rise of the practical sense in Europe was not only slow but uneven. Spurts of preoccupation with practical arts were followed by periods of stagnation or by a diversion of energies to other fields. During the High Middle Ages, in the wake of the Crusades, there was not only a marked expansion of commerce but also a striking increase in the use of waterwheels and windmills in manufacture; an increased proficiency in the mining, extraction and working of metals; and an expansion of arable land by clearing of forests and draining of marshes. The Black Death (1349), which killed off a third of the population, and the Hundred Years' War, which drained the resources of England and France, brought to an end a period which had some of the earmarks of an industrial revolution. The revival came in the fifteenth century and had its center in Italy and Germany. It saw not only the introduction of printing and paper and an unprecedented advance in the art of navigation, but a venturesomeness in all crafts and industries. This was a passionately creative age, and its practical activities consisted in more than mere adaptation of devices and practices from the Moslem world and the Far East. One has the feeling that the passionate pursuits of that age—the voyages of discovery; the pursuit of beauty, excellence, power, and pleasure; the bent for religious and social reforms; the pursuit of the practical—were all aspects of one and the same drive. The fading faith in a beyond released a fervent groping and searching for a heaven on earth. The explorers were looking for the lost paradise; beauty, excellence, power, and pleasure are the ingredients of an earthly paradise; the reformers were out to recast earthly life into a perfect shape; and the practical inventors tried to make the world over by work.

The wars in Italy between Spain and France, and the savage religious wars in Germany put a halt to this flourishing period. It was not until the end of the eighteenth century that the practical sense finally came into its own, and the modern Occident took up where the Late Neolithic craftsmen left off.

2

There is some evidence that the rise of the practical sense is linked with a diffusion of individual freedom. It is the "breath of democracy," as Bergson calls it, which urges the spirit of invention onward and gives it the necessary scope. The impulse to make use of every resource and device to facilitate and expand the world's work is lodged in the individual who is more or less on his own and has to prove his worth by his own work. Where compact collective unity blurs the awareness of individual separateness, the present is seen as a mere link between past and future and the details of everyday life as too trivial to bother with. This was as true of the Middle Ages as it is of contemporary collectivist societies. On the other hand, to the individual on his own, the present looms large and everyday affairs are the main content of life, and every undertaking is a test and a trial. He is eager to utilize everything within reach to advance his ends.

Wherever we find a quickening of the human spirit, we are perhaps justified in tracing it back to a situation in which the individual has been released, if but for a short time, from the dominance of the group—its observations, formulas and ideas. The significant point is that where such a situation occurs, its earliest phase is as a rule marked by an alertness to practical affairs. In most cases, the practical phase is of relatively short duration; it is terminated either by stagnation or by a diversion of energies to other fields.

There are indications that the outburst of practical ingenuity in the Near East during the Late Neolithic period was a function of individual activity. In both Mesopotamia and Egypt the era was marked by a conflict of unknown origin that shattered village communities, clans, and tribes, and filled the land with their debris. The cities which first took shape during this period, and which set the stage for the emergence of civilization, were probably to begin with places of refuge for the remnants of broken communal bodies. Such a conglomerate population was for a time without fixed traditions and customs, and during this fluid phase the individual had elbowroom to follow his bents and exercise his initiative. Civilization, as it evolved round temple and royal household, was an effort to impose collective compactness on a heterogeneous multitude and herd it back into the communal corral.

We come upon a somewhat similar situation toward the end of the second millennium B.C. This was a time of tumult and trouble on the eastern coast of the Mediterranean. Invasions and migrations churned and heaved whole populations in Greece, Asia Minor, Syria, and even in the Delta region of Egypt. Out of this turbulence eventually crystallized the city states of Greece, the Ionian settlements in Asia Minor, the Philistine towns on the coast of Palestine, Greek and Etruscan settlements in Italy, and the Phoenician colonies in North Africa and Spain. The practical phase of this period saw the introduction and spread of the phonetic alphabet, the diffusion of the technique of iron smelting, and the invention of coined money.

A peculiar variant of the situation is to be found in the emergence of a Moslem civilization in the wake of the Arab conquest. Here we have a release of the individual by conversion—a conversion that was more convenient than heartfelt. Millions of people found themselves, almost overnight, stripped of age-old traditions and practices without as yet being encased by a new orthodoxy. For the talented individual in particular, the conversion to Islam was the opening of the door to opportunity. Almost all the outstanding personalities of the Moslem renaissance were non-Arabs. They were Persians, Turks, Jews, Greeks, Berbers, and Spaniards. The bearers of the new culture, known as "the people of the pen," were so notoriously impious that orthodox Moslems refused to break bread with them.[*]

In its early phase, lasting two to three centuries, the Moslem civilization displayed a remarkable ingenuity in putting to practical use theories and processes borrowed from near and far. Paper factories, sugar refineries, manufactories of textiles, leather, glazed tile, steel, and chemicals dotted the Moslem world from Spain to Central Asia. For the first time there was a systematic employment of the waterwheel and windmill. Artesian wells were bored in North Africa and other semiarid regions, and there was a development of vast irrigation projects. The magnetic compass, the astrolabe, and Indian arithmetic were put to practical use. All crafts were in a flourishing state. Stagnation set in with a hardening of orthodoxy, and finally disintegration in the wake of the Mongol incursion in the East and the Christian reconquest in Spain.

The impulse toward practical application given by the Crusades was also the product of the individual's release from constraints and ties. The sight of the sun-drenched world of the Near East with its fabulous cities, its exotic fashions in dress and food, and its flamboyant everyday life must have stirred the feeling in many of the crusaders that the present was not the vale of tears and place of exile the Church had made it out to be. The observation of a thriving Moslem civilization in action could not but give birth to the realization that Europe, too, had possibilities. Still, the

---

[*] S. D. Goitein, *Jews and Arabs* (New York: Schocken Books, 1955), p. 104

mere contact with the Moslem world probably was not decisive. Byzantium and Spain had such a contact for centuries, yet it did not release in them an impulse toward experimentation and innovation. What counted more was the fact of movement—the pulling out of thousands of individuals from the familiar routine of a parochial world. The emergence of the autonomous individual is rarely the end result of a long process of social growth and maturing. Most often it is the result of chance or even catastrophe. The individual is separated from the group—he either emigrates or is cast out, left behind, or carried off. It would be difficult to exaggerate the role played by emigrants, exiles, and refugees in the awakening of the Western world. It is plausible for instance that if the Reformation was a crucial factor in the rise of the modern Occident, it was due less to the effect of its doctrines than to the fact that the religious persecutions it set in motion filled Western Europe with refugees and voluntary emigrants. The rise of the Netherlands to economic eminence in the sixteenth century was in no small degree due to the influx of exiles from Spain, Portugal, and France. Similarly, the foundations of England's industrial prowess were laid by exiles and emigrants—both Protestant and Catholic—from Spain, Portugal, France, and the Netherlands. America is a classical example of energy released by the influx of emigrants from the Old World, and the ceaseless movement of population inside the continent.

3

The question is: Why did not classical Greece, with its considerable individual differentiation and its appreciation of the present, canalize its intelligence and ingenuity into practical pursuits? Despite its breathtaking uniqueness, Greek civilization shared a contempt for practicalness with other civilizations. It believed that a preoccupation with practical affairs "renders the body, soul, and intellect of free persons unfit for the exercise of virtue."

The first answer to suggest itself is that what counts most in the rise of the practical sense is the extent of individualism. Where individualism is exclusive, as it was in Greece, the individual can prove his worth by leadership or by cultivating his talents rather than by work. The 30,000 autonomous individuals who set the tone in Athens did not have to spend their energies on the mechanics of everyday life because most of the work was done by some 200,000 slaves. On the other hand, in the Occident, where individualism is diffused in the mass, there is inevitably an intimate contact between the individual and the world's work, and he will use everything on earth and in heaven to advance his undertakings.

Still, this does not tell the whole story. The neglect of the practical in Greece was also due to the fact that it was a society in which the influence of the intellectual was paramount. There is considerable evidence of the intellectual's age-long hostility to the utilitarian point of view. The antagonism made itself felt at a very early stage in history—almost with the invention of writing. Writing was first developed in the Near East for a practical purpose: namely, to facilitate accounting in storerooms and treasuries. The earliest examples we have of writing are inventories and tallies. Writing was one of the crafts attached to the temple and royal household; but from the very beginning the men who practiced the craft of writing were in a category by themselves. The scribe, unlike the potter, weaver, carpenter, etc., did not produce anything tangible and of unquestioned usefulness. Furthermore, the scribe was from the beginning an adjunct of management rather than a member of the labor force. Inevitably, this special position induced in the scribe attitudes and biases which could not but have a profound effect on the outlook of any society in which he played a paramount role. His lack of an unequivocal sense of usefulness set his face against practicalness and usefulness as tests of worth. His penchant for exclusiveness, too, reinforced his antipractical bias.

Since the realm of the practical is probably the only one in which the common run of humanity have as much chance of attaining excellence as the educated, it was natural for the scribe to limit the proof of individual worth to fields inaccessible to the mass.

On the whole it seems to be true that where the equivalents of the intellectual constitute a dominant class there is little likelihood of ingenuity finding wide application in practical affairs. The inventiveness which now and then breaks through in such social orders is diverted into the fanciful, magical, and playful. Hero's steam engine was used to work tricks in temples and divert people at banquets. According to Plutarch, Archimedes considered the work of an engineer as ignoble and vulgar, and looked on his ingenious mechanical inventions as playthings. In Mandarin-dominated China the potent inventions of the magnetic compass, gunpowder, and printing hardly affected daily life. The compass was used to find a desirable orientation for graves; gunpowder was used to frighten off evil spirits; and printing was employed mainly to multiply amulets, playing cards, and paper money. The exceptional arithmetical achievements of the Brahmin intellectuals did not have the slightest effect on the management of practical affairs, nor did it occur to Buddhist intellectuals to use their ingenuity to lighten the burden of daily tasks. They invented the waterwheel not to mill grain but to grind out prayers. In the Occident, too, the elite of clerks during the Middle Ages, and the early humanists of the Renaissance, decried revolutionary innovations in the way of doing things. The humanists were hostile to the invention of printing and ignored the great geographical discoveries.

It is of interest that the intellectual's disdain of the practical seems to persist even when he is apparently up to his neck in purely practical affairs. In the Communist countries, the dominant intelligentsia is preoccupied with the highly practical task of industrializing a vast expanse of the globe's surface. Yet despite their fervor for factories, mines, powerhouses, etc., they are permeated with a disdain for the practical aspects of these works.

Their predilection is for the monumental, grandiose, spectacular, and miraculous. They have no interest in the merely useful, and it is not at all strange that they should have left the details of housing, food, clothing, and other components of everyday life in a relatively primitive state. Harrison E. Salisbury[*] was struck on his recent travels through Soviet Russia by the almost total absence of liaison between research and practical application. He found hardly one example of the close integration between research and industry so common in America. This was true even of agriculture. He saw only one great agricultural experiment station on the American model, and it was in Rumania. There professors worked self-consciously in the fields. They told Salisbury: "People call us Americans."

The exceptional prominence given to the practical in America stems partly from the fact that we have here, for the first time in history, a civilization that operates its economy and government, and satisfies most of its cultural needs without the aid of the typical intellectual. Perhaps the recent demonstration of the country's dependence for its defense and progress on pure science and the performance of scientific theoreticians might presage a lessening of the cult of the practical. Almost all recent pronouncements in praise of science and scientists have an undertone of deprecation of the merely practical. Here as in other things our world is just now coming full circle. In the seventeenth century, the military engineer Vauban was eulogized for bringing mathematics down from the stars and applying it to mundane affairs. Now, with the orbiting of manmade stars, our intelligence and ingenuity are being diverted from practical affairs and directed back to the skies.

---

[*] *To Moscow and Beyond* (New York: Harper & Brothers, 1960), p.136.

4

The anti-practical bias of the intellectual has been most strik-ingly displayed in the development of the art of writing.

As already mentioned, writing was invented to keep track of the income and outgo of wares. It originated not in houses of learning but in warehouses, and there is evidence that it was the trader who first conceived the idea of script. Tags and marks of ownership preceded clay tablets and papyrus rolls. But once writing came into the keeping of the scribe, he set his face against any simplification and practical perfection of tile art. For two millennia after its invention writing remained a cumbersome, complex affair the mastery of which required a lifetime of application. Indeed, where the influence of the scribe remained unchallenged, as it was in Egypt, Mesopotamia, and China, there is evidence of a retrograde evolution: a tendency to overburden writing with all manner of artificial inflections. In short, the scribe was not interested in the elaboration of a practical script but in keeping writing a prerogative of the privileged few. He had a vested interest in complexity and difficulty. The simplification of writing by the introduction of the phonetic alphabet was the work of outsiders—the Phoenician traders.

It is often stated that it was the economic background of Mesopotamia and Egypt—payment of tribute to the temple, and the management of a vast irrigation system—which gave rise to the invention of writing. Actually, the economic background by itself does not seem enough. The empire of the Incas had no writing although its economic situation was not unlike that of Mesopo-tamia and Egypt. Where a preliterate society succeeds in perfecting an all-embracing bureaucratic system there is little likelihood that it will hit upon the idea of script. The preliterate equivalent of the scribe neither looks for nor welcomes practical devices such as writing and coinage which would enormously simplify his task. He, too, has a vested interest in complexity and difficulty. What seems decisive for the appearance of writing is the presence of the free trader. We are told that "beyond local barter there was no trade in Inca times, since the movement and distribution of food and other commodities was controlled by the state." * By the same token we are justified in assuming the widespread presence of the free trader in Mesopotamia and the Delta region of Egypt during the Late Neolithic age.

In scribe-dominated Egypt the free trader was as rare as in the Inca Empire. "We do not meet the word 'merchant' until the second millennium B.C., when it designates the official of a temple privileged to trade abroad." ** Similarly in Mesopotamia the trade routes were for centuries the concern of the central government, and at all times the state had a tight control on trade. The Mesopotamian merchant, no matter how much he prospered, did not see himself as an independent agent and would not assert himself against the central power. In China, the free trader could assert himself only during the breakdown of the bureaucratic apparatus toward the end of the Chou dynasty.

We know less about the origins of the trader than we do about the origins of the scribe. But as we watch the present goings on inside the Communist world, the realization is forced upon us that trading is a form of self-assertion congenial to common people—a sort of subversive activity; undoctrinaire, unheroic, and uncoordinated, yet ceaselessly undermining and frustrating totalitarian domination. The trader probably did not initiate the downfall of the ancient totalitarian systems, but he was quick to lodge himself in any cracks which appeared in the monolithic walls, and did all he could to widen them. Thus despite his trivial motivation and

---

* G. H. S. Bushnell, *Peru* (New York: Praeger, 1957), p. 128.
** Henri Frankfort, *The Birth of Civilization in the Near East* (New York: Doubleday Anchor Books, 1956), p. 118. See also J. E. Manchip White, *Ancient Egypt* (New York: Thomas Y. Crowell Company, 1955), p. 124: "Coined money did not appear in Egypt until the Persians introduced the silver shekel of Darius."

questionable practices, the trader has been a chief agent in the emergence of individual freedom and, what concerns us here, the canalization of ingenuity and energies into practical application.

It is true that where the trader feels himself supreme he may become as ruthless as any other ruling class. The institution of slavery which rotted the fiber of the ancient world was promoted and perpetuated by the trader as much as by king, priest, and scribe. It is also true that in the past commerce settled into a traditional stagnant routine over long periods of time. But on the whole, trade has been a catalyst of movement and change, and of government by persuasion rather than by coercion. The trader has neither the words nor the venom to transmute his grievances into an absolute truth and impose it upon the world. In a trader-dominated society, the scribe is usually kept out of the management of affairs, but is given a more or less free hand in the cultural field. By frustrating the scribe's craving for commanding action, the trader draws upon himself the scribe's wrath and scorn, but unintentionally he also releases the scribe's creative powers. It was not a mere accident that the prophets, the Ionian philosophers, Confucius, and Buddha made their appearance in a period in which traders were conspicuous and often dominant. The same was of course true of the birth of the Renaissance, and of the growth of science, literature, and art in modern times.

In a scribe-dominated society, the trader is regulated and regimented off the face of the earth. When the scribe comes into power, he derives a rare satisfaction from tearing tangible things out of the hands of practical people and harnessing these people to the task of achieving the impossible, and often killing them in the process.

The toleration of the scribe in a trader-dominated society means of course the toleration of an articulate opposition capable of giving voice to grievances and breeding disaffection and revolt. Thus, until recently, the antagonism between trader and scribe has led to beneficent results—they cracked each other's monopoly.

The trader cracked the scribe's monopoly of learning by introducing the simplified alphabet and printing and by promoting popular education. On the other hand, the scribe has been in the forefront of every movement which set out to separate the trader from his wealth. In the process, both knowledge and riches leaked out to wider sections of the population.

8 · Jehovah and the Machine Age

I once heard a brilliant young professor of political science wonder what it would be like if one were to apply the law of the diffusion of gases to the diffusion of opinion. The idea seemed to him farfetched, yet he was eager to play with it.

It occurred to me, as I listened, that to a Galileo or a Kepler the idea would not have seemed at all fantastic. For both Galileo and Kepler really and truly believed in a God who had planned and designed the whole of creation—a God who was a master mathematician and technician. Mathematics was God's style, and whether it was the movement of the stars, the flight of a bird, the diffusion of gases, or the propagation of opinions—they all bore God's mathematical hallmark.

It sounds odd in modern ears that it was a particular concept of God that prompted and guided the men who were at the birth of modern science. They felt in touch with God in every discovery they made. Their search for the mathematical laws of nature was to some extent a religious quest. Nature was God's text, and the mathematical notations were His alphabet.

The book of nature, said Galileo, is written in letters other than those of our alphabet—"these letters being triangles, quadrangles, circles, spheres, cones, pyramids, and other mathematical figures." So convinced was Kepler that in groping for the laws that govern the motions of the heavenly bodies he was trying to decipher God's text, he later boasted in exaltation that God the author had to wait six thousand years for His first reader. Leonardo da Vinci paused in his dissection of corpses to pen a prayer: "Would that it might please the Creator that I were able to reveal the nature of man and his customs even as I describe his figure." Leonardo's interest in anatomy may have arisen from his work as an artist, but he was eventually driven mainly by the curiosity of the scientist and the mechanic. Living creatures were wondrous machines devised by a master mechanic, and Leonardo was taking them apart to discover how they were built and how they worked. By observing them and tinkering with them, man could himself become a maker of machines. One could perhaps eventually build a seeing mechanism, a hearing mechanism, a flying machine, and so on. The making of machines would be a second creation: man's way of breathing will and thought into matter.

The concept of God as a master mathematician and craftsman accounts perhaps for the striking difference between the revival of learning and the revival of science in the sixteenth and seventeenth centuries. Whereas the revival of learning was wholly dominated by the ideas and examples of antiquity, the revival of science, though profiting from Greek scientific writing, manifested a marked independence from the beginning. The vivid awareness of God's undeciphered text spread out before them kept the new scientists from expending their energies in the exegesis and imitation of ancient texts. In this case, a genuine belief in God was a factor in the emergence of intellectual independence.

It is of course conceivable that modern science and technology might have developed as they did without a particular conception of God. Yet one cannot resist the temptation to speculate on the significance of the connection. It is as if the Occident had first to conceive a God who was a scientist and a technician before it could create a civilization dominated by science and technology. It is perhaps not entirely so, though it has often been said, that man makes his God in his own image. Rather does he create Him in the image and his cravings and dreams—in the image of what man wants to be. God-making could be part of the process by which a society realizes its aspirations: it first embodies them in the conception of a particular God, and then proceeds to imitate that God. The confidence requisite for attempting the unprecedented is most effectively generated by the fiction that in realizing the new we are imitating rather than originating. Our preoccupation with heaven can be part of an effort to find precedents for the unprecedented.

For all we know, one of the reasons that other civilizations, with all their ingenuity and skill, did not develop a machine age is that they lacked a God whom they could readily turn into an all-powerful engineer. For has not the mighty Jehovah performed from the beginning of time the feats that our machine age is even now aspiring to achieve? He shut up the sea with doors and said: "Hitherto shalt thou come but no further; and here shall thy proud waves be stayed." He made pools of water in the wilderness and turned the desert into a garden. He numbered the stars and called them by name. He commanded the clouds, and told rivers whither to flow. He measured the waters in the hollow of His hand, and meted out the heavens with the span, and comprehended the dust in a measure and weighed the mountains in scales.

The momentous transition that occurred in Europe after the late Middle Ages was in some degree also a transition from the imitation of Christ to the imitation of God. The new scientists felt close to the God who had created the world and set it going. They stood in awe of Him, yet felt as if they were of His school. They were thinking God's thoughts, and whether they knew it or not aspired to be like Him.

The imitation of God was undoubtedly a factor in the release of the dynamism which marked the modern Occident from its birth, and set it off from other civilizations. Not only the new scientists, but the artists, explorers, inventors, merchants, and men of affairs felt that, in the words of Alberti, "men can do all things if they will." When Columbus exclaimed, "n mondo e poco!" he was expressing triumph rather than despair. The momentous discoveries and achievements implied a downgrading of God. For there is vying in imitation, and the impulse is to overtake and overcome the model we imitate. With its increased mastery over things, the Occident began to feel that it was catching up with God; that it was taming God's creation and making it subservient to a manmade world. The Occident was harking back to the generation of the flood that set out to storm the heavens and felt that "nothing will be restrained from them which they have imagined to do."

9 · Workingman and Management

T here are many of us who have been workingmen all our lives and, whether we know it or not, will remain workingmen till we die. Whether there be a God in heaven or not; whether we be free or regimented; whether our standard of living be high or low—I and my like will go on doing more or less what we are doing now.

This sober realization need not be unduly depressing to people who have acquired the habit of work and who, like the American workingman, have the ingredients of a fairly enjoyable life within their reach. Still, the awareness of being an eternal workingman colors one's attitudes; and it might be of some interest to indicate briefly what the relations between management and labor look like when seen from his point of view.

To the eternal workingman management is substantially the same whether it is made up of profit seekers, idealists, technicians, or bureaucrats. The allegiance of the manager is to the task and the results. However noble his motives, he cannot help viewing the workers as a means to an end. He will always try to get the utmost out of them; and it matters not whether he does it for the sake of profit, for a holy cause, or for the sheer principle of efficiency.

One need not view management as an enemy or feel self-righteous about doing an honest day's work to realize that things are likely to get tough when management can take the worker for granted; when it can plan and operate without having to worry about what the worker will say or do.

The important point is that this taking of the worker for granted occurs not only when management has unlimited power to coerce but also when the division between management and labor ceases to be self-evident. Any doctrine which preaches the oneness of management and labor—whether it stresses their unity in a party, class, race, nation, or even religion—can be used to turn the worker into a compliant instrument in the hands of management. Both Communism and Fascism postulate the oneness of management and labor, and both are devices for the extraction of maximum performance from an underpaid labor force. The preachment of racial unity facilitated the exploitation of labor in our South, in French Canada, and in South Africa. Pressure for nationalist and religious unity served, and still serves, a similar purpose elsewhere.

Seen from this point of view, the nationalization of the means of production is more a threat than a promise. For we shall be bossed and managed by someone, no matter who owns the means of production—and we can have no defenses against those who can tell us in all truth that we, the workers, own everything in sight and they, our taskmasters, are driving us for our own good. The battle between Socialism and Capitalism is to a large extent a battle between bosses, and it is legitimate to size up the dedicated Socialist as a potential boss.

One need not call to mind the example of Communist Russia to realize that the idealist has the making of a most formidable taskmaster. The ruthlessness born of self-seeking is ineffectual compared with the ruthlessness sustained by dedication to a holy cause. "God wishes," said Calvin, "that one should put aside all humanity when it is a question of striving for His glory." So it is better to be bossed by men of little faith, who set their hearts on toys, than by men animated by lofty ideals who are ready to sacrifice themselves and others for a cause. The most formidable

69

employer is he who, like Stalin, casts himself in the role of a representative and champion of the workers.

Our sole protection lies in keeping the division between management and labor obvious and matter-of-fact. We want management to manage the best it can, and the workers to protect their interests the best they can. No social order will seem to us free if it makes it difficult for the worker to maintain a considerable degree of independence from management.

The things which bolster this independence are not utopian. Effective labor unions, free movement over a relatively large area, a savings account, a tradition of individual self-respect—these are some of them. They are within the worker's reach in this country and most of the free world, but are either absent or greatly weakened in totalitarian states.

In the present Communist regimes, unions are tools of management, worker mobility is discouraged by every means, savings are periodically wiped out by changes in currency, and individual self-respect is extirpated by the fearful technique of Terror. Thus it seems that the worker's independence is as good an index as any for measuring the freedom of a society.

The question is whether an independent labor force is compatible with efficient production. For if the attitude of the workers tends to interfere with the full unfolding of the productive process, then the workingman's independence becomes meaningless.

It has been my observation for years on the docks of San Francisco that, while a wholly independent labor force does not contribute to management's peace of mind, it can yet goad management to perfect its organization and to keep ever on the lookout for more efficient ways of doing things. Management on the San Francisco waterfront is busy twenty-four hours a day figuring out ways of loading and discharging ships with as few men as possible.

Mechanization became marked on the waterfront after the organization of the present militant labor union in 1934. The forklift and the pallet board are in universal use. There are special machines for handling sugar, grain, cement, ore, and newsprint. New arrangements and refinements appear almost every day. Here nobody has to be told that management is continually on the job. Certainly, there are other factors behind this incessant alertness, and some of them play perhaps a more crucial role in the process of mechanization. But it is quite obvious that a fiercely independent labor force is not incompatible with efficient production.

Contrary to the doctrine propounded by some in the heyday of the Industrial Revolution, mechanization has not taught docility to "the refractory hand of labor." At least here on the docks we know that we shall manage to get our share no matter what happens. And it is a dull workingman who does not see in the machine the only key to the true millennium. For only mechanization can mitigate—if not cure—"the disease of work," as de Tocqueville calls it, which has tortured humanity since the first day of its existence. To me the advent of automation is the culmination of the vying with God which began at the rise of the modern Occident. The skirmish with God has now moved all the way back to the gates of Eden. Jehovah and His angels, with their flaming and revolving swords, are now holed up inside their Eden fortress, while the blasphemous multitude with their host of machines are clamoring at the gate. And right there, in the sight of Jehovah and His angels, we are annulling the ukase that with the sweat of his brow man shall eat bread.

It is true, of course, that the cleavage between management and labor is a source of strain and strife. But it is questionable whether tranquility is the boon it is made out to be. The late William Randolph Hearst shrewdly observed that "whatever begins to be tranquil is gobbled up by something that is not tranquil." The constant effort to improve and advance is neither automatic nor the result of a leisurely choice between alternatives. In human affairs, the best stimulus for running ahead is to have something we must run from. The chances are that the millennial society, where the wolf and the lamb shall dwell together, will be a stagnant society.

10 · Popular Upheavals in Communist Countries

One of the most remarkable things about the popular upheavals which have taken place in Communist countries since the death of Stalin is that hardly anyone in the West expected them. The completeness of our surprise is a measure of the awe in which we stand of the Communist evil. We seem convinced that it has a boundless power to shape and crush men's souls. It can make proud and brave men crawl on their bellies and confess the most fantastic and absurd crimes, and it can evoke in a population crushed by terror and stripped of all self-respect and integrity an almost religious dedication to fatherland and nation, and a readiness to die for their abusers and exploiters. We have witnessed again and again this miracle of perversion: the terrorized millions of a Communist regime proclaiming themselves in the vanguard of humanity, chanting the praises of their oppressors and hissing defiance at the outside world.

Still, the important point is that, despite the overpowering impression of the potency of the Communist evil, our statesmen and publicists should not have been so wholly unprepared for the post-Stalin turmoil in Eastern Europe. For there was enough plausible theory on hand not only to suggest the possibility of popular unrest behind the Iron Curtain but also to indicate in what countries the first signs were likely to manifest themselves.

I shall try to outline here very briefly the few theoretical considerations in question.

De Tocqueville in his researches into the state of society in France before the revolution of 1789 found that "a people which had supported the most crushing laws without complaint, and apparently as if they were unfelt, throws them off with violence as soon as the burden begins to be diminished." In other words, a popular uprising is less likely when oppression is crushing than when it is relaxed. He tried to explain this apparent contradiction by pointing out the connection between discontent and hope: "The evils which are endured with patience as long as they are inevitable, seem intolerable as soon as a hope can be entertained of escaping from them." Despair and misery are static factors. The dynamism of an uprising flows from hope and pride. Not actual suffering but the hope of better things incites people to revolt.

The remarkable thing is that though the connection between discontent and hope is often observed, it somehow fails to impress itself on the mind. This is probably due to a confusion of the two types of hope: the immediate and the distant. It is the around-the-corner brand of hope that prompts people to action, while the distant hope acts as an opiate. For—to quote Paul's Epistle to the Romans—"if we hope for what we see not, then do we with patience wait for it." The Communist regimes have made exaggerated use of the distant, pie-in-the-future type of hope to keep an abused population meek and patient. But it is obvious that such regimes are to some extent prisoners of their own ruthlessness. We are told that an absolutist Communist leadership can change its attitudes and policies from one extreme to another without the least regard to the reaction of the populace. Still there is one thing it cannot do without risk, and that is to relent and reform. De Tocqueville puts it rather strongly when he says that "nothing short of great political genius can save a sovereign who undertakes to relieve his subjects after a long period of oppression." Basing myself on de Tocqueville's observations, I suggested in 1950 that "a popular upheaval in Soviet Russia is hardly likely before the people get a real taste of the good life. The most dangerous

moment for the regime of the Politburo will be when a considerable improvement in the economic conditions of the Russian
masses has been achieved and the iron totalitarian rule somewhat
relaxed." * And again—the critical moment for the Communist
regimes will come "when they begin to reform, that is to say, when
they begin to show liberal tendencies." **

Actually, in the case of a modern totalitarian regime the inciting effect of such a relaxation is not enough. Other factors have to
be present if the impatience generated by the immediate hope is to
ripen into disaffection and revolt. The West had reason to expect
some manifestation of unrest behind the Iron Curtain when the
successors of Stalin showed signs of relaxing the totalitarian grip.
But it needed some familiarity with other factors in order to fore-
see where the stirrings of actual opposition were likely to show
themselves.

Individual resentment, however intense and widespread, is not
likely to lead to any sort of active resistance so long as the disaf-
fected cannot associate themselves in thought with some collective
body or movement. It has been proved again and again in recent
decades that the individual who stands wholly alone does not pit
himself against a totalitarian tyranny, no matter how poignant his
grievances and how confident he is of his own worth. His only
source of strength is in not being himself but part of something
mighty and eternal. The faith, pride, and desperate courage
required to defy an implacable totalitarian machine are generated
by such an identification. And since the secret police and the
mutual mistrust which pervades the population preclude the
existence of a dissident body or movement inside a Communist
regime, it follows that the emergence of active opposition will
depend on the possibility of an identification with something

---

* Eric Hoffer, *The True Believer* (New York: Harper & Brothers, 1951), p.
28
** ibid., p. 44.

impressive beyond the reach of the regime—something either in the outside world or in a glorious past.

Stalin was vividly aware of this fact, and he went to fantastic lengths to obviate the remotest possibility of an outside identification. He seemed to aim at nothing less than the "elimination" of the outside world—the blotting out of all awareness of humanity outside the Communist sphere. His brazen propaganda depicted non-Communist humanity as utterly miserable, depraved, and sterile, and on the brink of perdition: there was nothing in it deserving of admiration and reverence, nothing worth identifying oneself with.

The purpose of the Iron Curtain was less to prevent the infiltration of spies and agents into the Communist prison-lands than to intercept the thoughts and longings of the captive millions reaching out to the world outside. The uncompromising ban on all emigration—even of a few women married to foreigners—consigned the outer world as it were to a different planet. Stalin's murderous hostility toward the Titoist heresy and all existing Socialist organizations was largely motivated by his fear that they might serve as objects of identification for potentially dissident elements inside the Communist world. He even saw the association in thought of a few Jews with the tiny state of Israel as a threat, and set in motion a venomous anti-Zionist campaign to counteract it.

Now it is obvious that, of all the satellite countries, Eastern Germany occupied a special position with respect to outside identification. Not only did the Eastern Germans find it easy to identify themselves with the free and thriving Western part of their nation, but, thanks to the presence of West Berlin, they did not feel completely cut off from the rest of humanity. Only in East Germany, therefore, was the immediate hope, brought by the relaxation after Stalin's death, linked to a strong outside identification, and hence the greater likelihood there of discontent exploding into an actual uprising.

What of the other satellite countries?

It would be reasonable to assume that an outside identification would come easiest to the countries nearest the outside world. But what precisely is the glorious outside world that could serve as an object of identification for the discontented individual in Hungary, Czechoslovakia, and Poland? Freedom-loving humanity is too vague a concept; America is too distant and inarticulate, and perhaps too foreign; Western Europe, as it is now constituted, is too narrow and blemished to evoke longing and devotion in the isolated individual squirming under the all-seeing eyes of totalitarian jailkeepers.

It seems to me that the ideal object of identification for the people in the satellite countries is the vision of a united Europe: a closely federated subcontinent, beautiful and powerful, possessed of more talent, skill, and learning than any other part of the world, and with a history unequaled in brilliance and achievement. A Europe, moreover, in which people can work, study, teach, build, trade, travel, and play wherever they please, and feel at home everywhere. Compared with this vision, Russia is a global slum, Asia a graveyard, and America merely one more cause for pride—the handiwork of Europe's undesirables dumped on a virgin continent.

Such a vision, however, does not rise of itself. It must be projected and diffused by a vigorous movement in the non-Communist part of Europe—a movement that will claim every inch of European territory outside the strict frontiers of Russia proper, and know how to convey to the captive millions that they have not been abandoned, that Europe sees them as its own flesh and bone, and that the Communist usurpation is but a passing nightmare.

In the absence of such a movement there is little likelihood that outside identification can be a decisive factor in generating active resistance against Communist domination. As things are now, it is not the living but the dead who can put heart in the trapped millions and rally them to desperate defiance. The totalitarian brand of tyranny has perfected an awesome technique for stripping the individual of all material and spiritual resources which might bolster his independence and self-respect. It deprives him of every alternative and refuge—even that of silence or retreat into solitariness. Not only is he cut off from the outside world, but his fellow men around him—including relatives, friends, and neighbors—are a threat rather than a support. He stands alone and naked, deprived even of the magic of words to sustain him in his total aloneness. For Stalin has murdered all potent words, and drained the lifeblood out of "honor," "truth," "justice," "liberty," "equality," "brotherhood," "humanity." There remain only the eternal dead—the individual's indomitable ancestors whose blood runs in his veins and whose spirit is sealed in every cell of his body. We hear much about the dead hand of the past; but, as a matter of fact, the dead have had a hand in every renascence, and communion with them has been a source of unequaled strength in desperate situations. The savageries of militant nationalism have inclined us to see a nation's preoccupation with its history as a social vice or disease. But in the soul-corroding atmosphere of a Communist tyranny, fervent communion with proud, defiant ancestors is the only way in which the atomized individual can resist the awesome process which would turn him into submissive raw material that can be manipulated at will. And it is moving to see how in Hungary and Poland the omnipotent dead have put to naught a decade of relentless Communist effort, and claimed the fervent devotion of even those most susceptible to Communist black magic—namely, the young and the intellectuals.

In normal times it can perhaps be said: "Happy the nation that has no history." But when a Hitler and a Stalin bestride the world it fares ill with a people that has no defiant ancestors to commune with, and does not feel the throb of their indomitable spirit in its veins.

11 · Brotherhood

I t is easier to love humanity as a whole than to love one's neighbor. There may even be a certain antagonism between love of humanity and love of neighbor; a low capacity for getting along with those near us often goes hand in hand with a high receptivity to the idea of the brotherhood of men. About a hundred years ago, a Russian landowner by the name of Petrashevsky recorded a remarkable conclusion: "Finding nothing worthy of my attachment either among women or among men, I have vowed myself to the service of mankind." He became a follower of Fourier, and installed a phalanstery on his estate. The end of the experiment was sad, but what one might perhaps have expected: the peasants—Petrashevsky's neighbors—burned the phalanstery.

Some of the worst tyrannies of our day genuinely are "vowed" to the service of mankind, yet can function only by pitting neighbor against neighbor. The all-seeing eye of a totalitarian regime is usually the watchful eye of the next-door neighbor. In a Communist state love of neighbor may be classed as counter-revolutionary. Mao Tsetung counts it a sin of the liberals that they will not report the misdeeds of "acquaintances, relatives, schoolmates, friends, loved ones." To promote solidarity among neighbors is as good a way as any to block the diffusion of totalitarianism in a society.

The capacity for getting along with our neighbor depends to a large extent on the capacity for getting along with ourselves. The self-respecting individual will try to be as tolerant of his neighbor's shortcomings as he is of his own. Self-righteousness is a manifestation of self-contempt. When we are conscious of our worth-lessness, we naturally expect others to be finer and better than we are. We demand more of them than we do of ourselves, and it is as if we wished to be disappointed in them. Rudeness luxuriates in the absence of self-respect.

Now it is the tragedy of our time that the enormous shrinkage in distance, both geographical and social, that has made neighbors of all nations, races, and classes coincides with an enormous increase in the difficulties encountered by the individual in main-taining his self-respect. In the Communist part of the world, government policies are designed not only to eliminate actual and potential opponents but to turn the population into a plastic mass that can be molded at will. A Communist regime cannot tolerate self-respecting individuals who will not transgress certain bounds in dealing with their fellow men. Such individuals, even when few in number, render a population uncontrollable. "Every despotism," wrote the nineteenth-century philosopher Amiel, "has a specially keen and hostile instinct for whatever keeps up human dignity and independence."

This hostility is particularly pronounced in a despotism that is doctrinaire. Because of its professed faith in the irresistibility of the doctrine that supposedly shapes its course, such a despotism cannot be satisfied with mere obedience. It wants to obtain by coercion the type of consent that is usually obtained only by the most effective persuasion. This requires a population made up of individuals totally devoid of self-respect—individuals who will enthusiastically hate what they love, and love what they hate. This, as Boris Pasternak told us, is the one thing a Communist regime really wants.

Nor is it at present easy for the individual to maintain his self-respect in the non-Communist part of the world. In the under-developed countries the poignant awareness of backwardness keeps even the exceptional individual from attaining "the unbought grace of life" that is the true expression of an unconscious and an unquestioned sense of worth. Similarly, individual self-respect cannot thrive in an atmosphere charged with racial or religious discrimination. Both the oppressors and the oppressed are blemished. The oppressed are corroded by an inner agreement with the prevailing prejudice against them, while the oppressors are infected with the fear they induce in others. Finally, even in advanced and wholly egalitarian societies, millions of people are robbed of their sense of worth by unemployment, and by the obsolescence of skills as the result of revolutionary advances in technology.

Thus it seems that under the conditions current in the world at present, the nearer people get to each other, and the more alike they become, the dimmer grows their awareness of the oneness of mankind. The human image is clear to us when it is a silhouette against a distant horizon. When we come close so that we can look into a fellow man's eyes, we find there mirrored an image of ourselves, and we do not like what we see.

The unattainability of self-respect has other grave consequences. In man's life the lack of an essential component usually leads to the adoption of a substitute. The substitute is usually embraced with vehemence and extremism, for we have to convince ourselves that what we took as second choice is the best there ever was. Thus blind faith is to a considerable extent a substitute for the lost faith in ourselves; insatiable desire a substitute for hope; accumulation a substitute for growth; fervent hustling a substitute for purposeful action; and pride a substitute for unattainable self-respect. The pride that at present pervades the world is the claim that one is a member of a chosen group—be it a nation, race, church, or party. No other attitude has so impaired the oneness of the human species and contributed so much to the savage strife of our time.

Good will and peace have their roots in the conditions of the individual's existence. But the terrible fact seems to be that with our present standards of usefulness and worth there is no certainty that economic and social betterment can cure the individual's private ills. The new industrial revolution holds the promise of an unprecedented abundance for all, and there is a chance that in the free world the masses, though largely unemployed, will still get their share of the good things of life. But unless there is a radical change in our conception of what is useful, worthwhile, and efficient, it is hard to see how an economic millennium could possibly create optimal conditions for general tolerance and benevolence.

Under our scheme of values, affluence and leisure may well intensify the tendencies toward national and racial exclusiveness. It is not the overworked and underpaid who make up the ranks of the D.A.R., the Dixiecrats, and similar organizations here and elsewhere. In an indolent population living off the fat of the land, the vital need for an unquestioned sense of worth and usefulness is bound to find expression in an intensified pursuit of explosive substitutes.

At bottom, a country's efficiency must be measured by the degree to which it realizes its human potentialities. Industry, agriculture, and the exploitation of natural resources cannot be deemed efficient if they do not serve as a means for the realization of the intellectual, artistic, and manipulative capacities inherent in a population.

Now that the new industrial revolution is on the way to solving the problem of means, and we can catch our breath, it behooves us to remember that man's only legitimate end in life is to finish God's work—to bring to full growth the capacities and talents implanted in us. A population dedicated to this end will not necessarily overflow with the milk of human kindness, but it will not try to prove its worth by proclaiming the superiority and exclusiveness of its nation, race, or doctrine.

12 · Concerning Individual Freedom

It seems to be generally assumed that the maintenance of freedom within a society requires the presence of sturdy individuals ready and able to stand up for their rights. We are told that "Eternal vigilance is the price of liberty," and that "He alone merits liberty who conquers it afresh from day to day." How relevant are these assertions to everyday experience in a more or less free society? Does individual freedom owe its existence to individual militancy? Can a man really feel free who has to be eternally vigilant and must win his freedom anew each day?

Pascal maintained that we are made virtuous not by our love of virtue but "by the counterpoise of two opposite vices." It takes a vice to check a vice, and virtue is the byproduct of a stalemate between opposite vices. The same probably holds true of individual freedom: we are free not by our own power but by the counterpoise of two opposite powers. Individual freedom is the automatic byproduct of a drawn-out contest between more or less equal parties, factions, bodies, and so on. The quality of the contestants seems immaterial. A contest between two reactionary bodies can be as productive of individual freedom as a contest between a reactionary and a liberal party. If Poland is at present the country with the most individual freedom in the Communist world, it is due mainly to the fact that a powerful Communist party and a powerful Catholic Church—neither of which has any concern for individual freedom—are there pitted against each other in a more or less equal contest. The present situation in Poland echoes to some extent the situation which prevailed in the Occident toward the end of the Middle Ages when Church and State, each reaching out for total dominion, were engaged in a prolonged tug of war, thus unintentionally preparing the ground for the birth of civil liberty.

The growth of freedom in the Occident has been marked by a diversification and distribution of power. Starting out with a division between sacerdotal and secular power, there evolved in Western societies additional categories of power (political, economic, intellectual), subdivisions within each category (a multiplicity of churches, parties, and corporations, independent legislatures and courts, an antagonism between labor and management, and between intellectuals and men of action); and safeguards against the perpetuation of power (periodic elections, and periodic confiscations through income and inheritance taxes). The rise of totalitarianism in the twentieth century constitutes a sharp reversal of this characteristic Occidental tendency. Totalitarianism spells simplification: an enormous reduction in the variety of aims, motives, interests, human types, and, above all, in the categories and units of power. In a totalitarian state, power is of one kind and the defeated individual, no matter how outstanding, can find no redress.

It is clear, therefore, that the presence of an effective, organized opposition is a prerequisite of individual freedom. A society that in normal times cannot function adequately without unanimity is unfit for freedom. It is equally clear that the activities of an effective opposition and of free individuals subject the body social to considerable strain. A society must be in good working order and firmly anchored in a tradition of unity if it is to stand up under the ceaseless tug of parties and the willfulness of free individuals. Its government, economy, and the whole apparatus of everyday life must function smoothly and with a considerable degree of automatism. This means that a free society is also a skilled society. A wide diffusion of skills—technical, political, and social—not only makes it possible for a society to function adequately under strain, but also enables it to dispense with fervor and enthusiasm, which unavoidably blur individual autonomy, and to avoid the curtailment of freedom involved in excessive tutelage and supervision. In a genuinely free society, even extraordinary tasks can be accomplished by ordinary people in an ordinary way, and the social process can run at room temperature rather than at white heat. Finally, a society needs a large measure of affluence before it can allow its members the full play of their initiative and bents. It must be able to afford the waste inherent in a riot of trial and error. There can be no real freedom without the freedom to fail.

There is no doubt that individual freedom is an unequaled factor in the release of social energies, and particularly in the activation of ordinary people. "It infuses," says de Tocqueville, "throughout the body social an activity, a force, and an energy which never exist without it and which bring forth wonders." But this source of energy can be tapped only under special conditions: a society must be strong enough to support, and affluent enough to afford, individual freedom. It would thus be wholly unreasonable to expect a backward country to modernize itself in a hurry in an atmosphere of freedom. Its poverty, lack of skill, and its need for fervor and unity militate against it. In exceptional cases, like Puerto Rico and Israel, where capital and skills are available, rapid modernization is not incompatible with a considerable measure of individual freedom.

To some extent, the present dominant role of the intellectual in the modernization of backward countries also militates against the prevalence of individual freedom. Not only does the intellectual's penchant for tutoring, directing, and regulating promote a regimented social pattern, but his craving for the momentous is bound to foster an austere seriousness inhospitable to the full play of freedom. The intellectual "transforms the prosaic achievements of

society into Promethean tasks, glorious defeats, tragic epics." *
The strained atmosphere of an eternal drama working up toward a
climax and a crisis is optimal for heroes and saints but not for the
autonomous individual shaping his life to the best of his ability.
The chances are that should an advanced country come into the
keeping of the intellectual it would begin to show many of the
hectic traits which seem to us characteristic of a backward country
in the throes of awakening.

To the intellectual the struggle for freedom is more vital than
the actuality of a free society. He would rather "work, fight, talk,
for liberty than have it." ** The fact is that up to now the free
society has not been good for the intellectual. It has neither
accorded him a superior status to sustain his confidence nor made
it easy for him to acquire an unquestioned sense of social usefulness. For he derives his sense of usefulness mainly from directing,
instructing, and planning—from minding other people's business
—and is bound to feel superfluous and neglected where people
believe themselves competent to manage individual and communal
affairs, and are impatient of supervision and regulation. A free
society is as much a threat to the intellectual's sense of worth as an
automated economy is to the workingman's sense of worth. Any
social order that can function with a minimum of leadership will be
anathema to the intellectual.

The intellectual craves a social order in which uncommon
people perform uncommon tasks every day. He wants a society
throbbing with dedication, reverence, and worship. He sees it as
scandalous that the discoveries of science and the feats of heroes
should have as their denouement the comfort and affluence of
common folk. A social order run by and for the people is to him a
mindless organism motivated by sheer physiologism.

---

* Raymond Aron, *The Opium of the Intellectuals* (Garden City, New
York: Doubleday, 1957), p. xiv.
** Lincoln Steffens, *The Autobiography of Lincoln Steffens* (New York:
Harcourt Brace, 1931), p. 635.

13 · Scribe, Writer, and Rebel

I t is often stated that the invention of writing about 3000 B.C. marked an epoch in man's career because it revolutionized the transmission of knowledge and ideas. Actually, as I have said before, for many centuries after its invention writing served solely as a tool of bookkeeping and administration, and it was not until the first millennium B.C. that people began to write down their observations and thoughts. Nevertheless, the invention of writing had an immediate and fateful effect by giving rise to the class of the educated. Though the scribe started out as a craftsman, he found himself from the beginning associated not with the working force but with the supervisory personnel. In the tomb painting of Egypt, the scribe with his scroll and pen stands alongside the overseer with his whip—both facing the common folk who did the world's work. The career of a scribe became, therefore, an avenue by which common people could gain entrance into the privileged segment of society, and it inevitably drew unto itself talent and ambition which might have flowed into more practical crafts and occupations. Thus the invention of writing initiated a change in the direction of the flow of social energies, and such a change is a crucial event often characteristic of turning points in history.

Ever since the invention of writing, the educated minority has been a factor in social stability. Where the educated make common cause with those in power, there is little likelihood of social unrest and upheaval, since only the educated can supply the catalyst of words that turns grievances into disaffection and revolt. On the other hand, a ruling class of vigor and merit may be swept away if it does not know how to win and hold the allegiance of the educated. With few exceptions, wherever we find a long-lived social organization, there is either an absence of an educated class or a close alliance between the educated and the prevailing dispensation. This was true of Sumer with its scribes, Egypt with its literati, India with its Brahmins, China with its mandarins, Judaism with its rabbis and scholars, the Roman Empire with its Roman and Greek intellectuals, Byzantium with its kritoi and sekretoi, and the Catholic Church with its clerks. The Chinese sage Mo Ti said of the ruling classes of Chi and Chu that "they lost their empire and their lives because they would not employ their scholars." Stalin the Terrible echoed this truth when he said: "No ruling class can endure without its intelligentsia."

To win and hold the allegiance of the educated they must be given a chance to live purposeful and prestigious lives; and almost all long-lived social bodies solved the problem by absorbing the educated into bureaucratic hierarchies. Since he is not an actual producer, the scribe needs a clearly marked status to certify his worth, some connection with the world's work to prove his usefulness, and some arrangement of automatic promotion to give him a sense of growth. All these needs are ideally fulfilled by the status and function of a civil servant. Ensconced in his bureaucratic niche, the scribe looked at his world and saw that it was good. He had no grievances and dreamt no dreams.

2

At what point did the scribe make his appearance as a writer?

For centuries after the invention of writing the scribe exercised his craft solely in matters connected with his employment as a civil servant. He kept records, took dictation, copied documents and religious texts. Literature was the domain of bards and storytellers who no more thought of writing down their stock in trade than any other craftsmen would the secrets of their trade.

When we note the approximate dates at which literature made its first appearance in several of the ancient civilizations, we detect a certain regularity. In Egypt the earliest examples of literary writing are from the later pall of the third millennium B.C., the period of confusion which marked the breakdown of the Old Kingdom—the first catastrophic crisis since the birth of civilization. In Sumer, the oldest literary records are from the early part of the second millennium B.C., after the fall of the Third Dynasty of Ur—"the most glorious age of Sumer." Sir Leonard Woolley remarks on the strangeness of the fact "that the great days of the Third Dynasty of Ur have left virtually no trace of any literary record." It is only when the great age was brought to an abrupt end by the invading Amorites and Elamites that we find a period of genuine literary activity. It was then (around 2000 B.C.) that "Sumerian scribes took it in hand to record the glories of the great days that had passed away." * In Greece, written literature begins after the fall of the highly bureaucratized social organization of the Mycenean age, and in Palestine after the breakdown of the centralized Solomonic kingdom. Finally, in China literature begins in the sixth century B.C. during the chaotic period of "the contending states" which followed the dissolution of the Chou Empire.

---

* C. Leonard Woolley, *The Sumerians* (Oxford: The Clarendon Press, 1929), p. 178.

The recurring connection between social debacle and the birth of literature might suggest that it needed the apocalyptic spectacle of a world coming to an end to release the creative flow in the scribe. Still granting that he was deeply moved by the sight of an eternal order dissolving in violence and anarchy, it is questionable whether it was the spectacle as such, however soul-stirring, that started the scribe writing. The dissolution of the social order had a personal significance for the scribe, more so than for any other segment of the population. The aristocracy and the priesthood weathered the social breakdown without experiencing a radical change in their standing. Indeed, in Egypt and China the break-down of the Empire resulted in the creation of numerous feudal states in which the power and prestige of the aristocracy and the priesthood were unimpaired or even enhanced. The masses, submerged in age-long subjection, continued as they were irrespective of a change of masters. Not so the scribe: he who had been so snugly embedded in his bureaucratic berth, secure in his worth and usefulness, found himself suddenly abandoned and unemployed. We hear an echo of the scribe's "private ail" in one of the earliest examples of Egyptian literature written by the treasury official Ipuwer: "They pay taxes no more by reason of the unrest. ... The magistrates are hungry and suffer need. ... The storehouse is bare and he that kept it is stretched out on the ground. The splendid judgment hall, its writings are taken away, the secret place is laid bare ... public offices are opened and their lists are taken away. ... Behold the officers of the land are driven out through the land." *

Stripped of his official identity, the scribe not only reached out for a new role as sage, prophet, and teacher, but had a desperate need to shine again in the use of his skill with pen, stylus, or brush. Thus Neferrohn, "a scribe with cunning fingers. . . stretched out his hand to the box of writing materials and took him a scroll and pen-

---

* Adolph Erman, *The Literature of the Ancient Egyptians* (London: Methuen & Company, 1927), pp. 97-99.

and-ink case, and then he put in writing." He wrote: "Up my heart that thou mayest bewail this land whence thou are sprung. ... Rest not! Behold, it lieth before your face. ... The whole land hath perished, there is naught left, and the black of the nail surviveth not what should be there." [*] He goes on lamenting and admonishing in the manner of his contemporary Ipuwer.

In Palestine and Greece the social debacle coincided with a diffusion of literacy due to the introduction of the simplified alphabet. The increase in the number of literate persons at a time when there were only meager opportunities for their adequate employment added to the unrest. Amos, a shepherd, and Hesiod, a farmer, mastered the art of writing and were gripped by the impulse to instruct and admonish their fellow men.

In China, many of the hereditary scribe families sank into the masses during the period of social disintegration, and carried the art of writing with them. Confucius came from such a family. [**] It is often the descendants of families that have come down in the world who act as a creative ferment. The memory of past splendor is like fire in their veins and it is likely to leak out in romancing, philosophizing, and prophesying.

So long as the scribe was kept busy as a civil servant there was little likelihood that he would start writing. The creative impulse is often born of a thwarted desire for commanding action. It was the hankering after a busy, purposeful life which forced the energies of the disinherited scribe into creative channels. Once started, he used everything he could lay his hands on as grist for his mill, and began compiling collections of poetry, myths, legends, histories, proverbs, and so on.

---

[*] Adolph Erman, *The Literature of the Ancient Egyptians* (London: Methuen & Company, 1927), p. 112.
[**] Liu Wu-chi, *Confucius, His Life and Time* (New York: Philosophical Library, 1955), p. 27.

3

It should be obvious that the circumstances which started the scribe writing could have equally turned him into a sheer rebel. The revolutionary, whatever be his holy cause or ideology, is often a man thwarted in his consuming passion for purposeful and imposing action. "Next to love," wrote Bakunin, "action is the highest form of happiness." He may spend most of his life talking and arguing, but once he gets his chance he reveals himself as a superb man of action.

In Palestine and China, the writer and the revolutionary appeared simultaneously and were often embodied in the same person. The prophets, as Renan suggested, were the first radical journalists, while in China the roving bands of unemployed clerks that were a feature of the period of "the contending states" cultivated both literature and subversion. It has been alleged that Confucius was "inciting the feudal lords against each other in the course of his wandering from one state to another, with the intention of somewhere coming into power himself." * The scribe ancestry of the revolutionary manifests itself in the fact that when he comes into power he creates a social pattern ideally suited to the aspirations and talents of the scribe—a regimented social order planned, managed, and supervised by a horde of clerks.

Still, despite their common ancestry, there is a fundamental difference between the writer's and the rebel's attitude toward the word. To the genuine writer, the word is an end in itself and the center of his existence. He may dream of spectacular action and be lured to play an active role, but in the long run he does not feel at home in the whirl of a busy life. However imposing and successful his action, he feels in his innermost being that he is selling his birthright for a mess of pottage. It is only when the creative flow

---

* Wolfram Eberhard, *A History of China* (Berkeley: University of California Press, 1950), p. 38.

within him materializes in serried ranks of words that he feels at home in the world.

Not so the rebel: to him words remain a means to an end; and the end is action. His eyes remain fixed on the denied goal, and his energies keep pressing against the obstacle. He cannot derive a sense of fulfillment from the sheer manipulation of words, and inevitably drifts toward the zone where words turn into action. Ideas have significance for him only as a prelude to action. Theorizing, philosophizing, arid writing are a means for hurdling or exploding the obstacles on the road to action.

There is thus a certain antagonism between the writer and the revolutionary. In general it is probably true that by how much the writer is a revolutionary by so much less is he a writer. At bottom it is perhaps a question of inner endowment: the genuine writer can write his rebellion while the revolutionary can only live it. In the rare instances where outstanding capacities for revolutionary activity and for creativeness are present in the same person, the two capacities do not manifest themselves simultaneously. In Milton, Trotsky, Koestler, Silone, and others, writing came to the fore in periods of enforced or voluntary inaction. Trotsky knew that "Periods of high tension and social passions leave little room for contemplation and reflection. All the muses—even the plebeian muse of journalism in spite of her sturdy hips—have hard sledding in time of revolution." He also recognized that to a true rebel writing is an anemic substitute for action. In his *Diary in Exile*, Trotsky says of Lassalle that he would have gladly left unwritten what he knew if only he could have accomplished at least part of what he felt able to do, and he adds: "Any revolutionary would feel the same way."

4

Nothing is so unsettling to a social order as the presence of a mass of scribes without suitable employment and an acknowledged status. The spread of literacy in an illiterate society is, therefore, a critical process, and it has probably been an element in many turning points in history. Perhaps in retrospect the present convulsions in the underdeveloped countries will be seen mainly as the byproduct of a sudden increase in the number of literate persons. One hears a lot about the revolt of the masses but, aside from the rise of the United States, it would be difficult to point to a single historical development in which the masses were a prime mover and chief protagonist. Certainly, the present world crisis is not mass-made. Neither in the underdeveloped nor in the advanced countries are the masses restless, militant, and vainglorious. The explosive component in the contemporary scene is not the clamor of the masses but the self-righteous claims of a multitude of graduates from schools and universities. This army of scribes is clamoring for a society in which planning, regulation, and supervision are paramount and the prerogative of the educated. They hanker for the scribe's golden age, for a return to something like the scribe-dominated societies of ancient Egypt, China, and Europe of the Middle Ages. There is little doubt that the present trend in the new and renovated countries toward social regimentation stems partly from the need to create adequate employment for a large number of scribes. And since the tempo of the production of the literate is continually increasing, the prospect is of ever-swelling bureaucracies. Obviously, a high ratio between the supervisory and the productive force spells economic inefficiency. Yet where social stability is an overriding need, the economic waste involved in providing suitable positions for the educated might be an element of social efficiency.

It has been often stated that a social order is likely to be stable so long as it gives scope to talent. Actually, it is the ability to give scope to the untalented that is most vital in maintaining social stability. For not only are the untalented more numerous but, since they cannot transmute their grievances into a creative effort, their disaffection will be more pronounced and explosive. Thus the most troublesome problem which confronts social engineering is how to provide for the untalented and, what is equally important, how to provide against them. For there is a tendency in the untalented to divert their energies from their own development into the management, manipulation, and probably frustration of others. They want to police, instruct, guide, and meddle. In an adequate social order, the untalented should be able to acquire a sense of usefulness and of growth without interfering with the development of talent around them. This requires, first, an abundance of opportunities for purposeful action and self-advancement. Secondly, a wide diffusion of technical and social skills so that people will be able to work and manage their affairs with a minimum of tutelage. The scribe mentality is best neutralized by canalizing energies into purposeful and useful pursuits, and by raising the cultural level of the whole population so as to blur the dividing line between the educated and the uneducated. If such an arrangement lacks provisions for the encouragement of the talented, it yet has the merit of not interfering with them. We do not know enough to suit a social pattern to the realization of all the creative potentialities inherent in a population. But we do know that a scribe-dominated society is not optimal for the full unfolding of the creative mind.

14 · The Playful Mood

I have always felt that the world has lost much by not preserving the small talk of its great men. The little that has come down to us is marked by a penetration and a directness not usually conspicuous in formal discourse or writing; and one is immediately aware of its universality and timelessness. It seems strange that men should so effortlessly attain immortality in their playful moments. Certainly, some have missed immortality as writers by not writing as they talked. Clemenceau is a case in point. His books make dull and difficult reading, yet he could not open his mouth without saying something memorable. The few scraps we have of his small talk throw a more vivid light on the human situation than do shelves of books on psychology, sociology, and history. Toward the end of his life Clemenceau is reported to have exclaimed: "What a shame that I don't have three or four more years to live—I would have rewritten my books for my cook." It is also worth noting that the New Testament and the Lun Yu are largely records of impromptu remarks and sayings, and that Montaigne wrote as he spoke. ("I speak to my paper as I speak to the first person I meet.")

We are told that a great life is "thought of youth wrought out in ripening years"; and it is perhaps equally true that "great" thinking consists in the working out of insights and ideas which come to us in playful moments. Archimedes' bathtub and Newton's apple suggest that momentous trains of thought may have their inception in idle musing. The original insight is most likely to come when elements stored in different compartments of the mind drift into the open, jostle one another, and now and then coalesce to form new combinations. It is doubtful whether a mind that is pinned down and cannot drift elsewhere is capable of formulating new questions. It is true that the working out of ideas and insights requires persistent hard thinking, and the inspiration necessary for such a task is probably a byproduct of single-minded application. But the sudden illumination and the flash of discovery are not likely to materialize under pressure.

Men never philosophize or tinker more freely than when they know that their speculation or tinkering leads to no weighty results. We are more ready to try the untried when what we do is inconsequential. Hence the remarkable fact that many inventions had their birth as toys. In the Occident the first machines were mechanical toys, and such crucial instruments as the telescope and microscope were first conceived as playthings. Almost all civilizations display a singular ingenuity in toy making. The Aztecs did not have the wheel, but some of their animal toys had rollers for feet. It would not be fanciful to assume that in the ancient Near East, too, the wheel and the sail made their first appearance as playthings. We are told that in one of the oldest cemeteries in the world the skeletons showed that the average age of the population at death was less than twenty-five—and there is no reason to assume that the place was particularly unhealthy. Thus the chances are that the momentous discoveries and inventions of the Neolithic Age which made possible the rise of civilization, and which formed the basis of everyday life until yesterday, were made by childlike, playful people. It is not unlikely that the first domesticated animals were children's pets. Planting and irrigating, too, were probably first attempted in the course of play. (A girl of five once advised me to plant hair on my bald head.) Even if it could be shown that a striking desiccation of climate preceded the first appearance of herdsmen and cultivators, it would not prove that the conception of domestication was born of a crisis. The energies released by a crisis usually flow toward sheer action and application. Domestication could have been practiced as an amusement long before it found practical application. The crisis induced people to make use of things which amuse.

When we do find that a critical challenge has apparently evoked a marked creative response there is always the possibility that the response came not from people cornered by a challenge but from people who in an exuberance of energy went out in search of a challenge. It is highly doubtful whether people are capable of genuine creative responses when necessity takes them by the throat. The desperate struggle for existence is a static rather than a dynamic influence. The urgent search for the vitally necessary is likely to stop once we have found something that is more or less adequate, but the search for the superfluous has no end. Hence the fact that man's most unflagging and spectacular efforts were made not in search of necessities but of superfluities. It is worth remembering that the discovery of America was a byproduct of the search for ginger, cloves, pepper, and cinnamon. The utilitarian device, even when it is an essential ingredient of our daily life, is most likely to have its ancestry in the nonutilitarian. The sepulchre, temple, and palace preceded the utilitarian house; ornament preceded clothing; work, particularly teamwork, derives from play. We are told that the bow was a musical instrument before it became a weapon, and some authorities believe that the subtle craft of fishing originated in a period when game was abundant—that it was the product not so much of grim necessity as of curiosity, speculation, and playfulness. We know that poetry preceded prose, and it may be that singing came before talking.

On the whole it seems to be true that the creative periods in history were buoyant and even frivolous. One thinks of the lightheartedness of Periclean Athens, the Renaissance, the Elizabethan Age, and the age of the Enlightenment. Mr. Nehru tells us that in

India "during every period when her civilization bloomed, we find an intense joy in life and nature and a pleasure in the art of living." One suspects that much of the praise of seriousness comes from people who have a vital need for a facade of weight and dignity. La Rochefoucauld said of solemnity that it is "a mystery of the body invented to conceal the defects of the mind." The fits of deadly seriousness we know as mass movements, which come bearing a message of serious purpose and weighty ideals, are usually set in motion by sterile pedants possessed of a murderous hatred for festive creativeness. Such movements bring in their wake meager-mindedness, fear, austerity, and sterile conformity. Hardly one of the world's great works in literature, art, music, and pure science was conceived and realized in the stern atmosphere of a mass movement. It is only when these movements have spent themselves, and their pattern of austere boredom begins to crack, and the despised present dares assert its claims to trivial joys, that the creative impulse begins to stir amidst the grayness and desolation.

Man shares his playfulness with other warm-blooded animals, with mammals and birds. Insects, reptiles, etc., do not play. Clearly, the division of the forms of life into those that can play and those that cannot is a significant one. Equally significant is the duration of the propensity to play. Mammals and birds play only when young, while man retains the propensity throughout life. My feeling is that the tendency to carry youthful characteristics into adult life, which renders man perpetually immature and unfinished, is at the root of his uniqueness in the universe, and is particularly pronounced in the creative individual. Youth has been called a perishable talent, but perhaps talent and originality are always aspects of youth, and the creative individual is an imperishable juvenile. When the Greeks said, "Whom the gods love die young" they probably meant, as Lord Sankey suggested, that those favored by the gods stay young till the day they die; young and playful.

15 · The Unnaturalness of Human Nature

I n the early days of modern science we find outstanding scientists expressing their wonder and delight that the prodigious variety of nature should be the work of but few, simple laws. Galileo saw it as "a custom and habit of nature" to achieve its ends by means which are "common, simple, and easy." Kepler was convinced that "nature loves simplicity," and Newton wrote feelingly how "nature is pleased with simplicity and affects not the pomp of superfluous causes."

During the same period, the men whose preoccupation was with human nature spoke not of simplicity but of incredible complexity. Montaigne never wearied of expatiating on the inconstancy, lack of uniformity, involuteness, and unpredictability of human manifestations. It seemed to him that every bit in us plays every moment its own game, and that "there is as much difference between us and ourselves as between us and others." Pascal, a student of both nature and human nature, contrasted the simplicity of things with man's double and complex nature. He saw man as a mass of contradictions: an angel and a brute, a monster and a prodigy, the crown and scum of created things, the glory and scandal of the universe. Whatever harmony there is in us is "fantastic, changeable and various." He concluded that "men are of necessity so mad that not to be mad were madness in another form." He thought it quite in order that Plato and Aristotle should have written on politics as though they were laying down rules for a madhouse.

In the study of nature an explanation must not only be consistent with the facts, but also as simple and direct as possible. Where several explanations are advanced, the rule is followed that the one which is more simple is also more nearly correct. To choose the more complex explanation, says a recent writer on the nature of science, would be as sensible "as traveling eastward around the world to reach your neighbor's house which is next door to the west."

In human affairs the sensibleness of the direct, simple approach is by no means self-evident. Here it is often true that the simplest ends are reached only by the most roundabout and extravagant means. Even the predictable comes here to pass in unpredictable ways. To forget that man is a fantastic creature is to ignore his most crucial trait, and when contemplating human nature the wildest guesses and hunches are legitimate.

2

The fantastic quality of human nature is partly the product of man's unfinishedness. Being without specialized organs, man is in a sense a half-animal. He has to finish himself by technology, and in doing so he is a creator—in a sense a half-god. Again, lacking organic adaptations to a particular environment, he must adapt the environment to himself, and re-create the world. The never-ending task of finishing himself, of transcending the limits of his physical being, is the powerhouse of man's creativeness and the source of his unnaturalness. For it is in the process of finishing himself that man sloughs off the fixity and boundless submissiveness of nature.

The unnaturalness of human nature should offer a clue to the central meaning of man's ascent through the millennia: it was the result of a striving to break loose from nature and get out from under the iron laws which dominate it. The striving was not conscious, and it did not start from an awareness of strength. The process of reflection—of self-awareness—which fueled man's ascent was to begin with an awareness of helplessness: man the half-animal became poignantly aware of his unfinishedness and imperfection. He worshiped the more favored forms of life; worshiped their specialized organs, their skills and strength. He probably first killed animals, ate their flesh, and put on their skins, not to still his hunger and keep warm but to acquire their strength, speed, and skill, and become like them. Naked, unarmed, and unprotected, man clung desperately to an indifferent mother earth and passionately claimed kinship with her more favored children. But the discovery that he could create substitutes for the organs and inborn perfections which he lacked turned worship and imitation into a process of vying into a striving to overcome and overtake nature and leave it behind. By finishing and making himself man also remade the world, and the manmade world no longer clung to nature but straddled it. Instead of claiming kinship with other forms of life man now claimed a descent and a line apart, and began to see his uniqueness and dignity in that which distinguished him from the rest of creation.

Seen thus, the human uniqueness of an aspiration or an achievement should perhaps be gauged by how much it accentuates the distinction between human affairs and nonhuman nature; and it should be obvious that the aspiration toward freedom is the most essentially human of all human manifestations. Freedom from coercion, from want, from fear, from death are freedom from forces and circumstances which would narrow the gap separating human nature from nature and impose on man the passivity and predictability of matter. By the same token, the manifestation most inimical to human uniqueness is that of absolute power. The corruption inherent in absolute power derives from the fact that such power is never free from the tendency to turn man into a thing, and press him back into the matrix of nature from which he has risen. For the impulse of power is to turn every variable into a constant, and give to commands the inexorableness and relentlessness of laws of nature. Hence absolute power corrupts even when exercised for humane purposes. The benevolent despot who sees himself as a shepherd of the people still demands from others the submissiveness of sheep. The taint inherent in absolute power is not its inhumanity but its antihumanity.

3

To make of human affairs a coherent, precise, predictable whole one must ignore or suppress man as he really is, and treat human nature as a mere aspect of nature. The theoreticians do it by limiting the shaping forces of man's destiny to nonhuman factors: providence, the cosmic spirit, geography, climate, economic or physiochemical factors. The practical men of power try to eliminate the human variable by inculcating iron discipline or blind faith, by dissolving the unpredictable individual in a compact group, by subjecting the individual's judgment and will to a ceaseless barrage of propaganda, and by sheer coercion. It is by eliminating man from their equation that the makers of history can predict the future, and the writers of history can give a pattern to the past. There is an element of misanthropy in all determinists. To all of them man as he really is is a nuisance, and they strive to prove by various means that there is no such thing as human nature.

Even in the freest society power is charged with the impulse to turn men into precise, predictable automata. When watching men of power in action it must be always kept in mind that, whether they know it or not, their main purpose is the elimination or neutralization of the independent individual—the independent voter, consumer, worker, owner, thinker—and that every device they employ aims at turning man into a manipulatable "animated instrument," which is Aristotle's definition of a slave.

On the other hand, every device employed to bolster individual freedom must have as its chief purpose the impairment of the absoluteness of power. The indications are that such an impairment is brought about not by strengthening the individual and pitting him against the possessors of power, but by distributing and diversifying power and pitting one category or unit of power against the other. Where power is one, the defeated individual, however strong and resourceful, can have no refuge and no recourse.

There is no doubt that of all political systems the free society is the most "unnatural." It embodies, in the words of Bergson, "a mighty effort in a direction contrary to that of nature." Totalitarianism, even when it goes hand in hand with a modernization of technique, constitutes a throwback to the primitive, and a return to nature. It is significant that the "back to nature" movements since the day of Rousseau, though generous and noble in origin, have inevitably tended to terminate in absolutism and the worship of brute force.

Considering the complexity and unpredictability of man, it is doubtful whether effective social management can be based on expert knowledge of human nature. Societies are likely to function tolerably well either under a total dictatorship, which need not take human nature into account, or when least interfered with by government. Both absolute government and nominal government are ways of avoiding the necessity of having to deal with human nature.

4

Power, whether exercised over matter or over man, is partial to simplification. It wants simple problems, simple solutions, simple definitions. It sees in complication a product of weakness— the tortuous path compromise must follow.

Now, whereas in the realm of matter, the great simplifiers are the great scientists and technologists, in human affairs the great simplifiers are the great coercers—the Hitlers and Stalins. To some extent, Hitler and Stalin were scientists of man the way the physicist and the chemist are scientists of matter. Their policies and crimes were motivated as much by the scientist's predilection for simplification, predictability, and experimentation as by doctrinaire tenets or sheer malevolence. Even their murderous intolerance of dissenters had a "scientific" aspect: a dissenter is to the absoluteness of power what an exception is to the validity of a formulated scientific rule—both must be dealt with and somehow eliminated.

It is no coincidence that the men of absolute power in Soviet Russia have been so intrigued by the social implications of the Pavlovian experiments on dogs, and that concentration camps in Germany and Communist countries became factories of dehumanization, in which men were reduced to the state of animals, and were experimented on the way scientists experiment on rats and dogs. Absolute power produces not a society but a menagerie— even if it be what D'Argenson called a "menagerie of happy men."

It is an awesome thing that the most breathtaking example of daring we have witnessed in the second quarter of the twentieth century was the daring to think low enough of human beings. Both Hitler and Stalin displayed this daring in an unprecedented degree, and they caught the world unawares and almost overwhelmed it.

The full savor of power comes not from the mastery of nature but from the mastery of man. It is questionable whether he who can move mountains and tell rivers whither to flow has as exquisite a sense of power as he who can command the multitude and turn human beings into animated automata. Hence we find that a spectacular increase of man's power over nature is likely to be followed by a passionate attempt to master man—to use the power gained by victory over nature in the enslavement of men. Such a diversion is first discernible in the transition from the Late Neolithic age to the totalitarianism of the ancient river-valley civilizations. In the Near East, as pointed out earlier, the Late Neolithic age saw something like an industrial revolution; the era of civilization that followed was mainly preoccupied with the taming of man by coercion and magic.

The scientific and industrial revolution of modern times represents the next giant step in the mastery over nature; and here, too, an enormous increase in man's power over nature is followed by an apocalyptic drive to subjugate man and reduce human nature to the status of nature. Even where enslavement is employed in a mighty effort to tame nature, one has the feeling that the effort is but a tactic to legitimize total subjugation. Thus, despite its spectacular achievements in science and technology, the twentieth century will probably be seen in retrospect as a century mainly preoccupied with the mastery and manipulation of men. National-ism, Socialism, Communism, Fascism, militarism, cartelization and unionization, propaganda and advertising are all aspects of a general relentless drive to manipulate men and neutralize the unpredictability of human nature. Here, too, the atmosphere is heavy-laden with coercion and magic.

5

It was not the least part of the uniqueness of the ancient Hebrews that they were the first to enunciate a clear-cut separation between man and nature. In all ancient civilizations there was a feeling that a profound relationship existed between the things that happen in nature and the course of human affairs. The whole structure of magic was founded on the assumption of an identity between human nature and nature. The Hebrews were the first to reject any close ties or kinship between man and the rest of creation. Since their day, sun, stars, sky, earth, sea, rivers, plants, and animals have no longer been the seat of mysterious powers and the arbiters of man's fate. They have been but the handiwork of a one and only God who created both nature and man, yet made man in His own image—a fellow creator. Since the Hebrews, history rather than cosmic phenomena has been the meaningful drama of the universe.

The ancient Hebrews were also the first to demonstrate that man can defy and put to naught the law of the survival of the fittest which rules the rest of life. They set in motion an alchemy of the soul which transmutes elements of weakness into potent substitutes for all the attributes of the strong. They invented fanaticism, the distant hope, and boundless dedication; and equipped with these substitutes the weak not only survive but often confound the mighty.

On the whole, the unnaturalness of human nature is more strikingly displayed in the weak of the human species than in the strong. The strong are as a rule more simple, direct, and comprehensible—in a word, more natural. The indications are that in the process of tearing loose from nature it was the weak who took the first steps. Chased out of the forest by the strong, they first essayed to walk erect, and in the intensity of their soul first uttered words, and first grabbed a stick to use as weapon and tool. The weak's singular capacity for evolving substitutes for that which they lack suggests that they played a chief role in the evolvement of technology.

Man is most peculiarly human when he cannot have his way. His momentous achievements are rarely the result of a clean forward thrust but rather of a soul intensity generated in front of an apparently insurmountable obstacle which bars his way to a cherished goal. It is here that potent words and explosive substitutes have their birth, and the endless quest, and the stretching of the soul which encompasses heaven and earth.

Since it was man's unfitness—his being an outcast and an outsider on this planet—which started him on his unique course, it should not seem anomalous that misfits and outsiders are often in the forefront of human endeavor and the first to grapple with the unknown. The impulse to escape an untenable situation often prompts human beings not to shrink back but to plunge ahead. Moreover, it is in accord with the uniqueness of the human pattern that the misfits of the species should try to fit in not by changing themselves but by changing the world. Hence their bent for reform, innovation, tinkering, and plunging. Thus we find misfits in the vanguard of the settlement of new lands and the elaboration of new ways and methods in the economic, political, and cultural fields.

It is the unique glory of the human species that its rejected do not fall by the wayside but become the building stones of the new, and that those who cannot fit into the present should become the shapers of the future. Those, like Nietzsche and D. H. Lawrence, who see in the influence of the weak a taint that might lead to decadence and degeneration are missing the point. It is precisely the peculiar role played by its weak that has given the human species its uniqueness. One should see the dominant role of the weak in shaping man's fate not as a perversion of natural instincts and vital impulses, but as the starting point of the deviation which led man to break away from, and rise above, nature—not as degeneration but as the generation of a new order of creation.

The weak are not a noble breed. Their sublime deeds of faith, daring, and self-sacrifice usually spring from questionable motives. The weak hate not wickedness but weakness; and one instance of their hatred of weakness is hatred of self. All the passionate pursuits of the weak are in some degree a striving to escape, blur, or disguise an unwanted self. It is a striving shot through with malice, envy, self-deception, and a host of petty impulses; yet it often culminates in superb achievements. Thus we find that people who fail in everyday affairs often show a tendency to reach out for the impossible. They become responsive to grandiose schemes, and will display unequaled steadfastness, formidable energies and a special fitness in the performance of tasks which would stump superior people. It seems paradoxical that defeat in dealing with the possible should embolden people to attempt the impossible, but a familiarity with the mentality of the weak reveals that what seems a path of daring is actually an easy way out: it is to escape the responsibility for failure that the weak so eagerly throw themselves into grandiose undertakings. For when we fail in attaining the possible the blame is solely ours but when we fail in attaining the impossible we are justified in attributing it to the magnitude of the task.

The inept and unfit also display a high degree of venturesomeness in welcoming and promoting innovations in all fields. It is not usually the successful who advocate drastic social reforms, plunge into new undertakings in business and industry, go out to tame the wilderness, or evolve new modes of expression in literature, art, music, etc. People who make good usually stay where they are and go on doing more and better what they know how to do well. The plunge into the new is often an escape from an untenable situation and a maneuver to mask one's ineptness. To adopt the role of the pioneer and avant-garde is to place oneself in a situation where ineptness and awkwardness are acceptable and even unavoidable; for experience and know-how count for little in tackling the new, and we expect the wholly new to be ill-shapen and ugly.

Now, to point to the discrepancy between questionable motives and imposing achievements is not to decry humanity but to extol it. For the outstanding characteristic of man's creativeness is the ability to transmute petty and trivial impulses into momentous consequences. The alchemist's notion about the transmutation of metals is absurd with reference to nature, but corresponds to the actualities of human nature. There is in man's soul a flowing equilibrium between good and evil, the noble and the base, the sublime and the ridiculous, the beautiful and the ugly, the weighty and the trivial. To look for a close correspondence between the quality of an achievement and the nature of the motive which gave it birth is to miss a most striking aspect of man's uniqueness. The greatness of man is in what we can do with petty grievances and joys, and with common physiological pressures and hungers. "When I have a little vexation," wrote Keats, "it grows in five minutes into a theme for Sophocles." To the creative individual, all experience is seminal—all events are equidistant from new ideas and insights—and his inordinate humanness shows itself perhaps mainly in the ability to make the trivial and common reach an enormous way.

6

The significant fact is that the attributes which are at the root of man's uniqueness are also the main factors in the release of his creative energies. As we have seen, it was man's unfinishedness—his being an incomplete animal which started him on his unique course. This unfinishedness consists not only in the lack of specialized organs and organic adaptations, but also in the imperfection of man's instincts, and in an inability to grow up and mature. Now, each of these defects plays a vital role in the release of the creative flow. If the lack of specialized organs started the groping toward tools and weapons, then the lack of instinctual automatism introduced into man's behavior the seminal pause of hesitation. In animals, action follows on perception mechanically with almost chemical swiftness and certainty, but in man there is an interval of faltering and groping; and this interval is the seedbed of the images, ideas, means, aspirations, irritations, longings, and forebodings which are the warp and woof of the creative process. Finally, the retention of youthful characteristics in adult life endows man with a perpetual playfulness so fruitful of insights and illuminations.

It is to be expected that the pattern of unfinishedness should be most pronounced in the autonomous individual. Nothing on earth or in heaven is so poignantly and chronically incomplete as the individual on his own. In the individual totally integrated with others in a compact group, human uniqueness is considerably blurred. Fusion with others completes, stabilizes, and defuses. A compact collective body displays a submissiveness, predictability, and automatism reminiscent of nonhuman nature. Thus the emergence of the unattached individual must have been a crucial step in the attainment of human uniqueness. Yet the indications are that this step was not the end result of a slow process of social growth and maturing but the byproduct of catastrophe and disaster. The first individual was a lone survivor, a straggler, an outcast, a fugitive. Individual selfhood was first experienced not as something ardently wished for but as a calamity which befell the individual: he was separated from the group. All creative phases in history were preceded by a shattering or weakening of communal structures, and it was the individual debris who first set the creative act in motion. Fugitives seem to have been at the birth of everything new. They were the first free men, the first founders of cities and civilization, the first adventurers and discoverers; they were the seed of Israel, of Greece, of Rome, of America.

The severing of the individual from a compact group is an operation from which the individual never fully recovers. The individual on his own remains a chronically incomplete and unbalanced entity. His creative efforts and passionate pursuits are at bottom a blind striving for wholeness and balance. The individual striving to realize himself and prove his worth has created all that is great in literature, art, music, science, and technology. The individual, also, when he can neither realize himself nor justify his existence by his own efforts is a breeding cell of frustration and the seed of the convulsions which shake a society to its foundations.

These convulsions, being in essence a flight from the burdens of an individual existence, often terminate in totalitarian bodies dominated by absolute power.

It is a strangely moving spectacle this: the individual wearying of the burden of human uniqueness, shifting the load on his shoulders, and finally dropping it. For as he turns about to walk back, he finds himself one of a vast army with flags flying and drums beating, marching back to unbounded submissiveness and certitude—back to being a crumb of the rock of ages and an anonymous particle of a monolithic whole.

Yet it is part of the fantastic quality of man's nature that this passionate retreat should have often turned out to be but a stepping back preliminary to a leap ahead. In the modern Occident there has been a continuous tug of war between individualist and anti-individualist tendencies. The chauvinist and Socialist collectivism of the twentieth century is to the individualism of the nineteenth what Jacobinism was to the age of the Enlightenment and what the Reformation was to the Renaissance. And every time, until now, the resourceful Occidental individual somehow managed to re-assert himself and come out on top. He managed to convert the enthusiasm released by the anti-individualist movements into a stimulus of his own creative capacities, and an aid in his striving for self-realization and self-advancement. Thus we see again and again during the past four hundred years how the aftermath of every anti-individualist movement was marked by an outburst of individual creativeness in literature and art, and an upswing in individual venturesomeness and enterprise. It is true that the unprecedented ruthlessness displayed by contemporary anti-individualist drives makes one wonder whether this time, too, the individual will be able to come out on top. One wonders whether with their fearful instruments of coercion and control the contemporary mass movements may not at last succeed in bludgeoning he Occidental individuals for good into collectivist submissiveness.

7

Nothing so baffles the scientific approach to human nature as the vital role words play in human affairs. How can one deal with a physiochemical complex in which reactions are started and checked, accelerated and slowed down, by the sound or image of a word—usually a meaningless word?

It is of interest that the practice of magic where nature is concerned—the attempt to manipulate nature by words—rested on the assumption that nature is not unlike human nature, that methods of proven effectiveness in the manipulation of human affairs may be equally potent when applied to nonhuman nature. It can be seen that such an assumption is the mirror image of, and not infinitely more absurd than, the assumption implied in the scientific approach that human nature is merely an aspect of nature.

We know that words cannot move mountains, but they can move the multitude; and men are more ready to fight and die for a word than for anything else. Words shape thought, stir feeling, and beget action; they kill and revive, corrupt and cure. The "men of words"—priests, prophets, intellectuals—have played a more decisive role in history than military leaders, statesmen, and businessmen.

Words and magic are particularly crucial in time of crisis when old forms of life are in dissolution and man must grapple with the unknown. Normal motives and incentives lose then their efficacy. Man does not plunge into the unknown in search of the prosaic and matter-of-fact. His soul has to be stretched by a reaching out for the fabulous and unprecedented. He needs the nurse of magic and breathtaking fairytales to lure him on and sustain him in his faltering first steps. Even modern science and technology were not in the beginning a sober pursuit of facts and knowledge. Here, too, the magicians—alchemists, astrologers, visionaries—were the pioneers. The early chemists looked not for prosaic acids and salts but for the philospher's stone and the elixir of life. The early astronomers and discoverers, too, were animated by myths and fairytales. Columbus went looking not only for gold and fabulous empires but also for the Garden of Eden. When he saw the Orinoco, he was sure it was Gihon, one of the four rivers of Eden. He wrote back to Spain about all the tokens and virtues and mathematical calculations which forced him to the conclusion that "Paradise is to be found in these parts."

It is, indeed, questionable whether we can make sense of critical periods in history without an awareness of the role words and magic play in them. This is particularly true of the century we live in—a century dominated on the one hand by the scientific spirit and a superb practical sense, and on the other by the black magic of chauvinism, racialism, Fascism and Communism. The rapid transformation of millions of peasants into urban industrial workers, which often meant a leap from the Neolithic Age into the twentieth century, could not be realized without soul-stirring myths and illusions about an impending national, racial, or social millennium.

There is a widespread feeling at present that mankind has come to a fateful turning point. The feeling stems partly from the threat of a nuclear holocaust and partly from the fear that in a drawn-out contest with the Communist powers, we shall unavoidably be shaped in the image of the totalitarianism we loathe, and slay our hope even as we battle for it. More ominous perhaps are the signs that the weak of the species are about to be elbowed out of their role as pathfinders and shapers of the future. The new revolution in science and technology which has so enormously increased man's power over nature has also enormously reduced the significance of the average individual. With the advent of automation and the utilization of atomic energy, it might soon be possible for a relatively small group of people to satisfy all of a country's needs and fight its wars too without the aid of the masses. Man's destiny is now being shaped in fantastically complex and expensive laboratories staffed by supermen, and the new frontier has no place for the rejected and unfit. Instead of being the leaven of history and the mainspring of the ascending movement of man, the weak are likely to be cast aside as a waste product. One is justified in fearing that the elimination of the weak as shaping factors may mean the end of history—the reversion of history to zoology.

Yet there is the possibility that the weariness and dejection induced in us by the present crisis are clouding our vision and impairing our capacity for prognosticating the future. For even as we enumerate the forces which threaten to cast out the weak to outer darkness, there are things happening in every part of the globe which should make us pause, wonder, and hope. Precisely at this moment, we see everywhere backward countries—unimaginably poor in worldly goods, knowledge, and skill—awakening from a paralysis of centuries and vaulting themselves onto the stage of history to reenact the immemorable drama of the hindmost become foremost. This surely is a performance of the most poignant significance; and if we can savor its full import we shall not be discomfited by the crudity, arrogance, hostility, savagery, and hysteria of the performers. Our most ardent hope should be that this be not a last performance.

It is difficult to see how without an awareness of the unnaturalness of human nature one could make sense of the goings on in the underdeveloped parts of the world. Why should the sober, practical task of modernizing a backward country require the staging of a madhouse? Here certainly is an outstanding example of the fantastic discrepancy between means and ends often observed in human affairs. Incantations, myths, and preposterous illusions are required to release the energies which enable the weak to vault over or explode the obstacles athwart their path. The untrained and unequipped masses in the backward countries cannot be stirred to utmost effort by self-interest or logical persuasion. Nor can they be induced to learn and advance step by step. For learning is to them one more proof of their inadequacy, and a gradual advance but a flailing of the arms in the morass of the present. They want not a prosaic step ahead but a miraculous leap out of a mean present into a glorious future. They need the illusion that in trying to catch up tomorrow with other people's yesterdays they are actually running ahead and showing the way to the rest of mankind. The practical task of industrialization must figure as a momentous undertaking in the service of a holy cause. Potent words, communion with the faithful, and flaunting defiance are as essential as technical training, adequate equipment, and satisfactory food and housing. The backward masses clambering up the steep incline of history must see themselves as the vanguard of humanity, the bearers of a one and only truth, the chosen instrument of human destiny. The march out of their backwardness must be as the march of conquerors.

16 · The Role of the Undesirables

I n the winter of 1934, I spent several weeks in a federal transient camp in California. These camps were originally established by Governor Rolph in the early days of the Depression to care for single homeless unemployed of the state. In 1934, the federal government took charge of the camps for a time, and it was then that I first heard of them.

How I happened to get into one of the camps is soon told. Like thousands of migrant agricultural workers in California, I then followed the crops from one part of the state to the other. Early in 1934, I arrived in the town of El Centro, in the Imperial Valley. I had been given a free ride on a truck from San Diego, and it was midnight when the truck driver dropped me on the outskirts of El Centro. I spread my bedroll by the side of the road and went to sleep. I had hardly dozed off when the rattle of a motorcycle drilled itself into my head and a policeman was bending over me saying, "Roll up, mister." It looked as though I was in for something; it happened now and then that the police got overzealous and rounded up the freight trains. But this time the cop had no such thought. He said, "Better go over to the federal shelter and get yourself a bed and maybe some breakfast." He directed me to the place.

I found a large hall, obviously a former garage, dimly lit, and packed with cots. A concert of heavy breathing shook the thick air. In a small office near the door, I was registered by a middle-aged

117

clerk. He informed me that this was the "receiving shelter" where I would get one night's lodging and breakfast. The meal was served in the camp nearby. Those who wished to stay on, he said, had to enroll in the camp. He then gave me three blankets and excused himself for not having a vacant cot. I spread the blankets on the cement floor and went to sleep.

I awoke with dawn amid a chorus of coughing, throat clearing, the sound of running water, and the intermittent flushing of toilets in the back of the hall. There were about fifty of us, of all colors and ages, all of us more or less ragged and soiled. The clerk handed out tickets for breakfast, and we filed out to the camp located several blocks away, near the railroad tracks.

From the outside the camp looked like a cross between a factory and a prison. A high fence of wire enclosed it, and inside were three large sheds and a huge boiler topped by a pillar of black smoke. Men in blue shirts and dungarees were strolling across the sandy yard. A ship's bell in front of one of the buildings announced breakfast. The regular camp members—there was a long line of them—ate first. Then we filed in through the gate, handing our tickets to the guard.

It was a good, plentiful meal. After breakfast our crowd dispersed. I heard some say that the camps in the northern part of the state were better, that they were going to catch a northbound freight. I decided to try this camp in El Centro.

My motives in enrolling were not crystal clear. I wanted to clean up. There were shower baths in the camp and washtubs and plenty of soap. Of course I could have bathed and washed my clothes in one of the irrigation ditches, but here in the camp I had a chance to rest, get the wrinkles out of my belly, and clean up at leisure. In short, it was the easiest way out.

A brief interview at the camp office and a physical examination were all the formalities for enrollment. There were some two hundred men in the camp. They were the kind I had worked and traveled with for years. I even saw familiar faces—men I had worked with in orchards and fields. Yet my predominant feeling was one of strangeness. It was my first experience of life in intimate contact with a crowd. For it is one thing to work and travel with a gang, and quite another thing to eat, sleep, and spend the greater part of the day cheek by jowl with two hundred men.

I found myself speculating on a variety of subjects: the reason for their chronic belly-aching and beefing—it was more a ritual than the expression of a grievance; the amazing orderliness of the men; the comic seriousness with which they took their games of cards, checkers, and dominoes; the weird manner of reasoning one overheard now and then. Why, I kept wondering, were these men within the enclosure of a federal transient camp? Were they people temporarily hard up? Would jobs solve all their difficulties? Were we indeed like the people outside?

Up to then I was not aware of being one of a specific species of humanity. I had considered myself simply a human being—not particularly good or bad, and on the whole harmless. The people I worked and traveled with I knew as Americans and Mexicans, Whites and Negroes, Northerners and Southerners, etc. It did not occur to me that we were a group possessed of peculiar traits, and that there was something—innate or acquired—in our make-up which made us adopt a particular mode of existence.

It was a slight thing that started me on a new track.

I got to talking to a mild-looking, elderly fellow. I liked his soft speech and pleasant manner. We swapped trivial experiences. Then he suggested a game of checkers. As we started to arrange the pieces on the board, I was startled by the sight of his crippled right hand. I had not noticed it before. Half of it was chopped off lengthwise, so that the horny stump with its three fingers looked like a hen's leg. I was mortified that I had not noticed the hand until he dangled it, so to speak, before my eyes. It was, perhaps, to bolster my shaken confidence in my powers of observation that I now began paying close attention to the hands of the people around me. The result was astounding. It seemed that every other man had been mangled in some way. There was a man with one arm. Some men limped. One young, good-looking fellow had a wooden leg. It was as though the majority of the men had escaped the snapping teeth of a machine and left part of themselves behind.

It was, I knew, an exaggerated impression. But I began counting the cripples as the men lined up in the yard at mealtime. I found thirty (out of two hundred) crippled either in arms or legs. I immediately sensed where the counting would land me. The simile preceded the statistical deduction: we in the camp were a human junk pile.

I began evaluating my fellow tramps as human material, and for the first time in my life I became face-conscious. There were some good faces, particularly among the young. Several of the middle-aged and the old looked healthy and well-preserved. But the damaged and decayed faces were in the majority. I saw faces that were wrinkled, or bloated, or raw as the surface of a peeled plum. Some of the noses were purple and swollen, some broken, some pitted with enlarged pores. There were many toothless mouths (I counted seventy-eight). I noticed eyes that were blurred, faded, opaque, or bloodshot. I was struck by the fact that the old men, even the very old, showed their age mainly in the face. Their bodies were still slender and erect. One little man over sixty years of age looked a mere boy when seen from behind. The shriveled face joined to a boyish body made a startling sight.

My diffidence had now vanished. I was getting to know everybody in the camp. They were a friendly and talkative lot. Before many weeks I knew some essential fact about practically everyone.

And I was continually counting. Of the two hundred men in the camp, there were approximately as follows:

Cripples	30
Confirmed drunkards	60
Old men (55 and over)	50
Youths under twenty	10
Men with chronic diseases, heart, asthma, TB	12
Mildly insane	4
Constitutionally lazy	6
Fugitives from justice	4
Apparently normal	70

(The numbers do not tally up to two hundred since some of the men were counted twice or even thrice—as cripples and old, or as old and confirmed drunks, etc.)

In other words: less than half the camp inmates (seventy normal, plus ten youths) were unemployed workers whose difficulties would be at an end once jobs were available. The rest (60 percent) had handicaps in addition to unemployment.

I also, counted fifty war veterans, and eighty skilled workers representing sixteen trades. All the men (including those with chronic diseases) were able to work. The one-armed man was a wizard with the shovel.

I did not attempt any definite measurement of character and intelligence. But it seemed to me that the intelligence of the men in the camp was certainly not below the average. And as for character, I found much forbearance and genuine good humor. I never came across one instance of real viciousness. Yet, on the whole, one would hardly say that these men were possessed of strong characters. Resistance, whether to one's appetites or to the ways of the world, is a chief factor in the shaping of character; and the average tramp is, more or less, a slave of his few appetites. He generally takes the easiest way out.

The connection between our make-up and our mode of existence as migrant workers presented itself now with some clarity.

The majority of us were incapable of holding onto a steady job. We lacked self-discipline and the ability to endure monotonous, leaden hours. We were probably misfits from the very beginning. Our contact with a steady job was not unlike a collision. Some of us were maimed, some got frightened and ran away, and some took to drink. We inevitably drifted in the direction of least resistance—the open road. The life of a migrant worker is varied and demands only a minimum of self-discipline. We were now in one of the drainage ditches of ordered society. We could not keep a footing in the ranks of respectability and were washed into the slough of our present existence.

Yet, I mused, there must be in this world a task with an appeal so strong that were we to have a taste of it we would hold on and be rid for good of our restlessness.

My stay in the camp lasted about four weeks. Then I found a haying job not far from town, and finally, in April, when the hot winds began blowing, I shouldered my bedroll and took the highway to San Bernardino.

It was the next morning, after I got a lift to Indio by truck, that a new idea began to take hold of me. The highway out of Indio leads through waving date groves, fragrant grapefruit orchards, and lush alfalfa fields; then, abruptly, passes into a desert of white sand. The sharp line between garden and desert is very striking. The turning of white sand into garden seemed to me an act of magic. This, I thought, was a job one would jump at—even the men in the transient camps. They had the skill and the ability of the average American. But their energies, I felt, could be quickened only by a task that was spectacular, that had in it something of the miraculous. The pioneer task of making the desert flower would certainly fill the bill.

Tramps as pioneers? It seemed absurd. Every man and child in California knows that the pioneers had been giants, men of boundless courage and indomitable spirit. However, as I strode on across the white sand, I kept mulling over the idea.

Who were the pioneers? Who were the men who left their homes and went into the wilderness? A man rarely leaves a soft spot and goes deliberately in search of hardship and privation. People become attached to the places they live in; they drive roots. A change of habitat is a painful act of uprooting. A man who has made good and has a standing in his community stays put. The successful businessmen, farmers, and workers usually stayed where they were. Who then left for the wilderness and the unknown? Obviously those who had not made good: men who went broke or never amounted to much; men who though possessed of abilities were too impulsive to stand the daily grind; men who were slaves of their appetites—drunkards, gamblers, and women chasers; outcasts—fugitives from justice and ex-jailbirds. There were no doubt some who went in search of health—men suffering with TB, asthma, heart trouble. Finally there was a sprinkling of young and middle-aged in search of adventure.

All these people craved change, some probably actuated by the naive belief that a change in place brings with it a change in luck. Many wanted to go to a place where they were not known and there make a new beginning. Certainly they did not go out deliberately in search of hard work and suffering. If in the end they shouldered enormous tasks, endured unspeakable hardships, and accomplished the impossible, it was because they had to. They became men of action on the run. They acquired strength and skill in the inescapable struggle for existence. It was a question of do or die. And once they tasted the joy of achievement, they craved for more.

Clearly the same types of people which now swelled the ranks of migratory workers and tramps had probably in former times made up the bulk of the pioneers. As a group the pioneers were probably as unlike the present-day "native sons"—their descendants—as one could well imagine. Indeed, were there to be today a new influx of typical pioneers, twin brothers of the forty-niners, only in modern garb, the citizens of California would consider it a menace to health, wealth, and morals.

With few exceptions, this seems to be the case in the settlement of all new countries. Ex-convicts were the vanguard in the settling of Australia. Exiles and convicts settled Siberia. In this country, a large portion of our earlier and later settlers were failures, fugitives, and felons. The exceptions seemed to be those who were motivated by religious fervor, such as the Pilgrim Fathers and the Mormons.

Although quite logical, the train of thought seemed to me then a wonderful joke. In my exhilaration, I was eating up the road in long strides, and I reached the oasis of Elim in what seemed almost no time. A passing empty truck picked me up just then and we thundered through Banning and Beaumont, all the way to Riverside. From there I walked the seven miles to San Bernardino.

Somehow, this discovery of a family likeness between tramps and pioneers took a firm hold on my mind. For years afterward it kept intertwining itself with a mass of observations which on the face of them had no relation to either tramps or pioneers. And it moved me to speculate on subjects in which, up to then, I had had no real interest, and of which I knew very little.

I talked with several old-timers—one of them over eighty and a native son—in Sacramento, Placerville, Auburn, and Fresno. It was not easy, at first, to obtain the information I was after. I could not make my questions specific enough. "What kind of people were the early settlers and miners?" I asked. They were a hardworking, tough lot, I was told. They drank, fought, gambled, and wenched. They wallowed in luxury, or lived on next to nothing with equal ease. They were the salt of the earth.

Still it was not clear what manner of people they were.

If I asked what they looked like, I was told of whiskers, broad-brimmed hats, high boots, shirts of many colors, sun-tanned faces, horny hands. Finally I asked: "What group of people in present-day California most closely resembles the pioneers?" The answer, usually after some hesitation, was invariably the same: "The Okies and the fruit tramps."

I tried also to evaluate the tramps as potential pioneers by watching them in action. I saw them fell timber, clear firebreaks, build rock walls, put up barracks, build dams and roads, handle steam shovels, bulldozers, tractors, and concrete mixers. I saw them put in a hard day's work after a night of steady drinking. They sweated and growled, but they did the work. I saw tramps elevated to positions of authority as foremen and superintendents. Then I could notice a remarkable physical transformation: a seamed face gradually smoothed out and the skin showed a healthy hue; an indifferent mouth became firm and expressive; dull eyes cleared and brightened; voices actually changed; there was even an apparent increase in stature. In almost no time these promoted tramps looked as if they had been on top all their lives. Yet sooner or later I would meet up with them again in a railroad yard, on some skid row, or in the fields—tramps again. It was usually the same story: they got drunk or lost their temper and were fired, or they got fed up with the steady job and quit. Usually, when a tramp becomes a foreman he is careful in his treatment of the tramps under him; he knows the day of reckoning is never far off.

In short it was not difficult to visualize the tramps as pioneers. I reflected that if they were to find themselves in a single-handed life-and-death struggle with nature, they would undoubtedly display persistence. For the pressure of responsibility and the heat of battle steel a character. The inadaptable would perish, and those who survived would be the equal of the successful pioneers.

I also considered the few instances of pioneering engineered from above—that is to say, by settlers possessed of lavish means, who were classed with the best where they came from. In these instances, it seemed to me, the resulting social structure was inevitably precarious. For pioneering deluxe usually results in a plantation society, made up of large landowners and peon labor, either native or imported. Very often there is a racial cleavage between the two. The colonizing activities of the Teutonic barons in the Baltic, the Hungarian nobles in Transylvania, the English in Ireland, the planters in our South, and the present-day plantation societies in Kenya and other British and Dutch colonies are cases in point. Whatever their merits, they are characterized by poor adaptability. They are likely eventually to be broken up either by a peon revolution or by an influx of typical pioneers—who are usually of the same race or nation as the landowners. The adjustment is not necessarily implemented by war. Even our old South, had it not been for the complication of secession, might eventually have attained stability without war: namely, by the activity of its own poor whites or by an influx of the indigent from other states.

There is in us a tendency to judge a race, a nation, or an organization by its least worthy members. The tendency is manifestly perverse and unfair; yet it has some justification. For the quality and destiny of a nation are determined to a considerable extent by the nature and potentialities of its inferior elements. The inert mass of a nation is in its middle section. The industrious, decent, well-to-do, and satisfied middle classes—whether in cities or on the land—are worked upon and shaped by minorities at both extremes: the best and the worst.

The superior individual, whether in politics, business, Industry, science, literature, or religion, undoubtedly plays a major role in the shaping of a nation. But so do the individuals at the other extreme: the poor, the outcasts, the misfits, and those who are in the grip of some overpowering passion. The importance of these inferior elements as formative factors lies in the readiness with which they are swayed in any direction. This peculiarity is due to their inclination to take risks ("not giving a damn") and their propensity for united action. They crave to merge their drab, wasted lives into something grand and complete. Thus they are the first and most fervent adherents of new religions, political upheavals, patriotic hysteria, gangs, and mass rushes to new lands.

And the quality of a nation—its innermost worth—is made manifest by its dregs as they rise to the top: by how brave they are, how humane, how orderly, how skilled, how generous, how independent or servile; by the bounds they will not transgress in their dealings with a man's soul, with truth, and with honor.

The average American of today bristles with indignation when he is told that this country was built, largely, by hordes of undesirables from Europe. Yet, far from being derogatory, this statement, if true, should be a cause for rejoicing, should fortify our pride in the stock from which we have sprung.

This vast continent with its towns, farms, factories, dams, aqueducts, docks, railroads, highways, powerhouses, schools, and parks is the handiwork of common folk from the Old World, where for centuries men of their kind had been beasts of burden, the property of their masters—kings, nobles, and priests—and with no will and no aspirations of their own. When on rare occasions one of the lowly had reached the top in Europe, he had kept the pattern intact and, if anything, tightened the screws. The stuffy little corporal from Corsica harnessed the lusty forces released by the French Revolution to a gilded state coach, and could think of nothing grander than mixing his blood with that of the Hapsburg masters and establishing a new dynasty. In our day a bricklayer in Italy, a house painter in Germany, and a shoemaker's son in Russia have made themselves masters of their nations; and what they did was to re-establish and reinforce the old pattern.

Only here, in America, were the common folk of the Old World given a chance to show what they could do on their own, without a master to push and order them about. History contrived an earth-shaking joke when it lifted by the nape of the neck lowly peasants, shopkeepers, laborers, paupers, jailbirds, and drunks from the midst of Europe, dumped them on a vast, virgin continent and said: "Go to it; it is yours!"

And the lowly were not awed by the magnitude of the task. A hunger for action, pent up for centuries, found an outlet. They went to it with ax, pick, shovel, plow, and rifle; on foot, on horse, in wagons, and on flatboats. They went to it praying, howling, singing, brawling, drinking, and fighting. Make way for the people! This is how I read the statement that this country was built by hordes of undesirables from the Old World.

Small wonder that we in this country have a deeply ingrained faith in human regeneration. We believe that, given a chance, even the degraded and the apparently worthless are capable of constructive work and great deeds. It is a faith founded on experience, not on some idealistic theory. And no matter what some anthropologists, sociologists, and geneticists may tell us, we shall go on believing that man, unlike other forms of life, is not a captive of his past—of his heredity and habits—but is possessed of infinite plasticity, and his potentialities for good and for evil are never wholly exhausted.

Former migratory worker and longshoreman, Eric Hoffer burst on the scene in 1951 with his irreplaceable tome, *The True Believer*, and assured his place among the most important thinkers of the twentieth century. Nine books later, Hoffer remains a vital figure with his cogent insights to the nature of mass movements and the essence of humankind.

Photograph by George Knight

Hoffer in the old San Francisco Public Library

Of his early life, Hoffer has written: "I had no schooling. I was practically blind up to the age of fifteen. When my eyesight came back, I was seized with an enormous hunger for the printed word. I read indiscriminately everything within reach—English and German.

"When my father (a cabinetmaker) died, I realized that I would have to fend for myself. I knew several things: One, that I didn't want to work in a factory; two, that I couldn't stand being dependent on the good graces of a boss; three, that I was going to stay poor; four, that I had to get out of New York. Logic told me that California was the poor man's country."

Through ten years as a migratory worker and as a gold-miner around Nevada City, Hoffer labored hard but continued to read and write during the years of the Great Depression. The Okies and the Arkies were the "new pioneers," and Hoffer was one of them. He had library cards in a dozen towns along the railroad, and when he could afford it, he took a room near a library for concentrated thinking and writing.

In 1943, Hoffer chose the longshoreman's life and settled in California. Eventually, he worked three days each week and spent one day as "research professor" at the University of California in Berkeley. In 1964, he was the subject of twelve half-hour programs on national television. He was awarded the Presidential Medal of Freedom in 1983.

CPSIA information can be obtained
at www.ICGtesting.com
Printed in the USA
BVHW070310051220
594771BV00008B/321